WRITING POETRY

THE WRITERS NEWS LIBRARY OF WRITING

Vol 1 WRITING
Make the Most of Your Time
Kenneth Atchity

Vol 2 START WRITING TODAY!
Creative Writing for Beginners
André Jute

Vol 3 PRACTICAL NOVEL WRITING
Dilys Gater

Vol 4 KEEP ON WRITING!
From Creative Writer to Professional Writer
André Jute

Vol 5 SHORT STORY WRITING
Dilys Gater

Vol 6 SUCCESSFUL ARTICLE WRITING
Gillian Thornton

Vol 7 WRITING PROPOSALS & SYNOPSES THAT SELL
André Jute

Vol 8 HOW TO WRITE FOR CHILDREN
Marion Hough

Vol 9 WRITING POETRY
Doris Corti

WRITING POETRY

Doris Corti

WRITERS NEWS

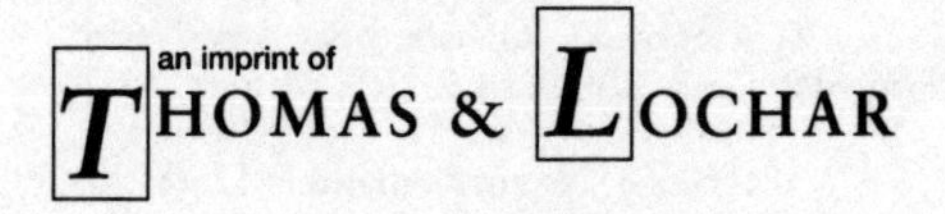

For my husband, who coped

British Library Cataloguing in Publication Data
Corti, Doris
Writing Poetry. – ("Writers News"
Library of Writing; Vol. 9)
I. Title II. Series
808.1
ISBN 1 85877–001–7 (hb)
1 85877–002–5 (pb)

Typeset by XL Publishing Services, Nairn
Printed in Great Britain by BPC Wheatons Ltd, Exeter
For David St John Thomas Publisher,
PO Box 4, Nairn, Scotland IV12 4HU

Contents

FOREWORD

This book is not merely an objective study of the devices and techniques used in poetry. It incorporates in fourteen chapters practical ways and ideas of how to structure emotions. The ideas it contains should prove invaluable to the beginner, as well as the more established poet.

1
In The Beginning

In the beginning there is the emotion and the instinct that drives one on to write a poem. Instinct is the prime motivator when starting to write poetry, for we write out of experiences not in order to communicate information. Dramatic events, personal and often emotional, as well as scenes from nature can all produce that first image. It is most likely the writer who sees and thinks in pictures who will concentrate on poetry.

It is often a slight thing that nudges instinct. A sudden realisation of the truth about something, an immediate recognition of what had before been unrecognisable. A frown on someone's face, or a quickly concealed look of resentment. A glimpse of love, or the opposite, seen in a person's eyes. Something that had been considered familiar, a face, a building, a flower, a group of people, a room, a view, can quite suddenly take on a different aspect. When the familiar seems to change, we view it with different eyes because a known reality appears to change. An image might spring to mind, or a phrase, perhaps the opening line, or merely two or three words can herald the arrival of a poem.

It is this beginning that must be recorded, so we start by writing our response to a change (real or imagined) that we see in a person, or in a situation. Or we might write a vivid description of something that has made an impression on us, and the emotion that this has created. Triumphantly we begin a new poem, the basis of which is the emotive experience that precipitated it. We each have different thought processes, different memories, and because of this our choice of methods to capture an experience will also be different.

Writing a poem is to go down a long path of self-exploration. A poem is a realisation of something discovered, not merely through something external, but within oneself. It is as though the picture hanging in a room, and grown familiar to us, suddenly takes on new perspectives through hitherto unseen curves, lines, and shadows.

What is being related to readers within a poem is the idea that provoked it into being a poem. A poem is the vehicle by which the poet presents something in an exact way to convey feelings. The poet chooses to do this by presenting thoughts, ideas, emotions or descriptions through the structure of the poem. This structure can be developed through the choice of language, form and patterns. It is the way these are used that will make a reader's mind connect with the primary instinct that first persuaded the poet to write the poem.

For example in the following sonnet which observes the Shakespearean pattern, the theme is 'mourning'. The triumphant ending however, and the restrained emotion within the poem, which is controlled by the structure, enables the readers to be immensely moved.

...For Spring by J. Woodcock

Deep midwinter, and the slanting rain.
The sexton's spade blunted by frozen ground.
All's done. Walk steadily away again.
Wreaths almost camouflage the quiet mound.
A scavenging fox, half unseen in the fog,
Claws down the dustbin at her cottage door,
Tumbling her trowel, her garden catalogue,
Dumped rubbish no one wanted any more.

Deep, deep in her garden, planted long ago –
Before the invading nettles, tall couch-grass –
Forgotten bulbs, buried far under the snow,
Are urgent with living, as the slow months pass.
At last, through rotted leaves, spring sunshine spills
New light on reincarnation: her daffodils.

The poem follows a regular pattern which is extremely functional, it is clear and precise in its message, and never strays into a less than coherent statement. It has a quiet and deliberate pace, and the words which have been carefully selected to reinforce this are used effectively. This measured pace, and the conciseness of the form, helps readers to identify with the emotive quality within the poem.

It is not necessary to concentrate on strictness of form, rhythm or rhyme when a poem first comes to mind. It is necessary however, to keep returning to the poem over a certain time, say two or three weeks, and to read the poem with a fresh mind, to analyse it and be judgmental.

Poems that appear to have a perfectly natural flow, do so because the poet has used judgment and discipline. It is an immature poet who allows an outpouring of emotion to be the dominant factor. The difficulty is finding the dividing line between outpouring, and suppression.

Writing a poem is a long and often arduous process, because there has to be a waiting time. The poem has to be put out of sight, and brought out at certain periods to be read again in an observant way. Naturally, the poet will be checking for the usual things that get overlooked in the first draft, like punctuation and grammatical errors, but also to note if the intensity of emotion is restrained yet still prominent.

In the beginning it was personal thought and experience that motivated the writing of a poem. The start of it, will be an exploration of this personal element. Whether we are aware of it or not, a poem is a self-exploratory process. It is, however, essential to lose the subjective viewpoint even when sharing an emotion. It is possible, by creating verbal images and using other methods, which will be explained in the following chapters, to evoke a response in a reader.

Poets have to decide if their language embellishes the essence or emotion within a poem, and to choose the form which is considered best to persuade the reader to enter into the experience, scene or viewpoint, that the poet is describing. Often it is a combination of language and correct choice of form, as well as other devices, that helps sustain the first impulse of the poem.

The pattern chosen, or the form of the poem, as well as the language selected, very rarely comes from a logical thought process. The first basic idea nags, so the poet is eager to put it down in words. This captures an impression, but much work is necessary to complete the poem. All sentimentality has to be avoided, unnecessary words taken out, and consideration of the regularity of rhyme and rhythm (if used) taken into account. In fact, until the reality of the idea being written about is both seen and felt, by poet and reader alike, the poem has to be continually worked upon. If this is not done, the poem will become merely a vehicle for self-expression. Poetry demands more than an egotistical outpouring of personal thoughts. It insists that we emphasise in the best possible ways the small moment, incident, experience, scene or character that moved the poet to write.

It is the poet's obligation to persuade readers to identify with the event or experience being written about. It is not enough to describe or simply talk about them. A response has to be evoked in a reader, and to do this, a poet's thoughts and language have to be structured. This does not mean restricting language to what is often thought of – mistakenly – as being poetic. The use of archaic language, or clichéd phrases, does not make real poetry, it is merely poeticism. Imagery too can be less than convincing, if it is not thought about carefully. Learning to structure our emotions can be an all absorbing task in every poem we write but, by learning to understand methods and devices used to emphasise major points, the task may well become less arduous and more enjoyable.

A poem can never be rushed. When the poem has been written out (and that first impetuous rush of ideas must be written down or they will be lost) it must be put aside for at least a few days. After this interval, look at it again and read it aloud. Consider how any pattern or device (however small) either improves it or detracts from the impetus that caused it to be written. The pattern may perhaps be the use of a small rhyme on the end of lines. It maybe a line comes to mind, that has a number of words that all start with the same letter, it may be the use of a repetitive phrase, words, or simply one word.

Bad poetry can be seen when a poem uses language and devices that are showy, superficial, crude or naive. If certain technicalities are used with control by the poet, then a poem will have strength, depth, and subtleness of expression.

Technicalities: that does rather make it sound as though poetry is being contrived, but this does not follow. Once the technical points or devices (one has to call them something) are used, there is an excitement created, as the poet manipulates the first impulse or idea into a structure that best defines it.

A short poem by contemporary poet Phil Carradice is concise, by letting go the restriction of a strict metrical pattern on each line, and creating emphatic images, he persuades his readers to feel the emotive point within the poem:

Burma Star by P. Carradice

When I was little, knee high
to an ice cream van, I wore
a cowboy suit with blazing
buckskin fringes –
a regular Roy Rogers!

My father, smiling, pinned his Burma Star,
his other bronze medallions
across my pigeon chest.
Like sheriff's stars I wore them.

I lost the medals, spinning,
falling in a graceful arc,
cut down by phantom gunmen from
a wild, imaginary west.

My father shrugged
and rubbed my hair
and for an instant, in his eyes,
I saw real soldiers coughing
blood red death within the dark
and steaming jungles
of his past.

A simple method of structuring has been chosen. First of all, the way the poem is phrased pushes the images forcefully into our minds.

There is a deliberate use of the letter *s* which sets up an internal rhythm in the poem. Note particularly the last three lines of the first stanza, while the second stanza uses this letter intensively throughout, and on into the first line of the third stanza.

We are made aware in the opening line that the incident referred to, took place when the poet was a child. Those two words *knee high* bring the image of being small to mind, as do the words *pigeon chest*.

It has not been necessary for the poet to describe the father, who is made real by describing his actions: *Pinned his Burma Star* and *rubbed my hair*. Ordinary actions these, but of significance to the child, and this significance is made real to the reader of the poem. We, as the readers, are made to see what the child suddenly became aware of. He *for an instant* saw a changed look in the father's eyes: *real soldiers coughing blood red death within the dark and steaming jungles*. The last line is very forceful, it illustrates how the child is made aware that all these things happened in his father's past.

The whole story contained in the poem is held in a tightly knit structure, there is comparisons within the poem of the childhood of the poet's past, and the war-filled past of his father.

The structure of this poem is not based on metrical patterns, it is laid out in short lines that persuade you to read it at a fast pace. This suits the subject matter, for the poem is a short sharp incident, two minutes of life encompassed in the lines. The use of imagery, directness of statement, assonance and alliteration, bring rhythm and emotive power to the poem.

When a poem is well structured like this, it reads easily from the page, and glides into our minds. A poem may well begin as an emotive outlet, but by structuring it, it is the emotive essence only that becomes the cornerstone, and not the outpourings of our own emotions.

Emotion does not lack strength if it is under control. By the use of rhyme, rhythm, vowel patterning, syllable counting, interesting layout, and a number of other ploys, a poet can challenge the perceptions of the reader and display maturity in his writing. Overstated emotions are not only embarrassing, but we cheapen genuine feelings by describing emotions in words that are merely fatuous.

It is depth of expression that we are striving for when we

write a poem, and the vital quality of our work is diminished if our words evoke purely sentimental reactions.

In her poem *The Reading*, Barbara Rennie refers to the reading given by Irina Ratushkinskaya after being released from a Russian labour camp. The poem is a good example of structure being developed through the careful selection of vowels. These are used in appropriate places to emphasise the emotional impact the reading made on the poet:

The Reading by B. Rennie
(Irina Ratushkinskaya London 12 May 1987)

Fern frond branding
bright spear
of green
on the black sheath
of her dress.

She standing
straight
and brave
in front of us.
Slight.
And her fragility
defiant
declaring:
'No. I'm not afraid.'

But braver still
that
two lines from the end
admission: 'It's not
true. I am afraid.'
And that fear
sears
her courage for ever
into
the understanding
of the listening world.

Note the words *spear*, *green* and *sheath* in the first stanza. These extend the *e* sounds and make the pace slower, giving an effective pause on the images. The poet directs the form, using one word on a line occasionally to lead the reader into the inner depths of the poem. This highlights the fear of the newly released poet, by establishing that it is painful, that it *sears* and the significance is emphasised by placing that word on its own in a line.

Internal rhyming and alliterative rhythms control certain areas of the poem, as for instance *standing straight* and again in *defiant declaring*.

Without making any obvious overstatement, or losing control of the emotional impact, the poet has successfully drawn us into her feelings.

With words, we are able to describe, illustrate, argue, and draw imaginative pictures. The form that a poem takes may be dictated by words. A poem often seemingly starts from nowhere, although of course it may well have been held in our memory bank for years, or it may stem from a slight incident. If the words springing to mind seem to be the start of a line consisting of some intense pattern then the form of a poem may be arriving within a defined metrical sequence. Jot the words down immediately. They may not be in any grammatical order, but perhaps they are highlighting the incident being written about.

A rhyme coming in a few lines, started the following poem by a student at a poetry workshop:

The room resembles her,
it crackles in late winter sun,
and polished windows reflect the ritual hours
the tidying, and scrubbing floors,

now we observe the funeral cars and flowers.

These lines were simply written down, as the poem began to arrive. Before the student came to the workshop the poem had developed a little in the following way:

The room resembles her,
polished windows reflect the ritual hours
a sense of purpose in each swish of broom,
the scent of beeswax in every room.

We edge procession-wise towards funeral cars,
observing the clean furniture, and flowers.

It is obvious from these first few lines that the poem had first come to mind and was retained by the small pattern of rhyme and slant rhymes as in *hours* and *floors*, and *broom* and *room*. The poem had come to a decided halt and the student, a young girl, was confused. The storyline of the poem was about someone she knew, a relative, and she had wanted to explain why this relative had become a recluse.

She was advised not to worry unduly about the rhyming pattern: this had given her the idea of the poem but was now obscuring her thought process. It would be better, she decided, if she followed the rhythm of the vowels that seemed here and there to form another pattern. She found that two more lines came to mind later:

Her life was neatly parcelled up,
and sealed with a secret knot.

Counting the beats (or syllables) of these two lines we discovered another pattern. It appeared she did not require the use of a definite rhyming pattern at all, and eventually the poem became this:

Rituals

The room resembles her,
gleaming in late winter sun. We edge procession-wise
towards the funeral cars, along scrubbed floors,
passing polished windows that reflect ritual hours

of her life, neatly parcelled up
and sealed with a secret knot.

We recall the story told by family and friends,
of how her lover died on some muddy battlefield
since then, small rituals fixed a pattern in her days

a sense of purpose in each swish of broom,
and polish layered into floors. No time for idle talk
or smiles, nor to grow a rose
or any flower in garden's edge.

She kept her life uncoloured, and her dreams untold.
Gently we place the wreaths upon her grave,
like some apology.

The poem had eventually achieved what it set out to do, record the life of a certain character who chose to live a solitary existence. The poet in this particular case found the poem arriving through a rhyming pattern. If the words without any set pattern come to mind, then still write them down to capture the incident or idea occurring to you. Afterwards you may find that the patterning of vowels forms a rhythm, creates an echo, or through some kind of action creates an internal structure to the poem.

Also take note of the consonants and of the consonants surrounding vowels. Take for example *strange* and *fat*: as we say these two words our mouths move differently, and the difference in sound would be noticeable in a line of poetry:

In a strange land by a clear sea, and a green line
of hills, a fat ant sat…
for a moment, examining the sand.

Notice how the lines change rhythm; we stretch our mouths for the words *strange land* but not so much for *fat ant sat*. These last three words we say quickly, just as the ant moves quickly. The syllables in the word *examining* slow the pace again, which shows how a poet can manipulate words to achieve certain results.

The choice of how to structure a poem is for the poet to make. It often leads to despair when, having written a poem in one form, it does not seem to excite or move the reader in any way. It often helps at this point to read the poem aloud to fellow poets, at a workshop or creative writing class. The fault may well be pinpointed by someone outside the emotion experienced by the poet. Being too closely involved with the words and ideas can often inhibit the writer from conveying the true dramatic and honest sense of the original idea. It is easy to believe that what you wrote during the composition period was the best description of something or someone, and that the language, shape and form cannot be improved upon.

A form may well be dictated by the pattern of the words as they come to mind, or it may be selected by the poet as the best medium for emphasising a point vital to the understanding of the poem.

The following poem developed through repetitions of lines that kept occurring to me. The form evolving was a Villanelle, this and other forms are fully explained in chapter five. It can be seen that the lines that kept repeating themselves in my poem are the ones creating its strict pattern.

Over the years poets have used the Villanelle in its traditional form, and have also adapted it to suit their own work. It is a form in which the repetitive words and lines help to evoke atmosphere. In my poem you can hear, if reading aloud, how the emotive quality has been heightened by using a repetitive pattern as the poem's structure:

By the Pricking of My Thumbs

I have come to know the hour before dawn,
When shrouded familiars reach for my soul
In hidden shapes and shadows on the lawn.

Gaunt trees like knuckled hands from witches torn
Emerge grotesquely from the night's dark bowl;
I have come to know the hour before dawn.

Small animals cry out beneath the moon,
Predators wait to play their frightening role
In hidden shapes and shadows on the lawn.

My thumbs are pricking in the silent room
Primeval fears steal through my mind's dark hole,
I have come to know the hour before dawn.

The curtains stir, old terrors are reborn
In screech of owl, and dying cry of vole,
In hidden shapes and shadows on the lawn.

I wait, thumbs pricking by the cold hearth stone
For the dark angel, and the bell to toll.
I have come to know the hour before dawn,
In hidden shapes and shadows on the lawn.

Certain repetitive phrases give voice to the underlying apprehension and imagery is included for the same effect. You will find examples in the second line of the first stanza: *shrouded familiars* and the repetitive line of *In hidden shapes and shadows on the lawn*. The word *hidden* is intended to convey fear, and the word *shrouded* has connotations of death.

These (and other) words were chosen to emphasise the emotive force of the poem, while the form of the Villanelle provides the main structure.

Atmosphere can be created by imaginative use of words, and by the repetition of certain lines. It can also be enhanced by the use of metrical patterns. Alfred, Lord Tennyson, used both repetition and a strict metrical pattern known as the dactylic (more about metre in chapter four). An example is *Half a league, half a league...* in which each word *half* is accented. This example is a well known line from his famous *Charge of The Light Brigade*. The repetition is obvious, and the rhythm creates the impression of a trotting horse, achieved by the accented and unaccented words.

There are many devices which can help order and structure a poem, and these will be discussed in this book.

In the following poem several methods are used to emphasise the subject matter. The metrical pattern is the steady beat of the iambic, and the poet has also used a rhyming pattern that gently controls the structure and is exactly right for the theme. Alliteration, scattered throughout the poem with delicate touches, achieves a musical note, which again enhances the general theme of music.

Music by J.M. Stevens

Enchant my vision with your violin
That resurrects the young, remembered Springs;
Bring me the rain-rough clover, all the thin
High meadow calls, the swift, sky-piercing wings.

Chill me with trumpets; let me close my eyes
To see defeated legions in my brain,
The dripping silks, the fierce cloud streamered skies,
The pennants slitting crimson through the rain.

Play softly on the oboe; fretted ferns
Unravel in dark hedges of my grief
That yet is ecstasy. A sea-bird turns
To fall down wind, a star, a stone, a leaf.

But when you set your instruments apart,
Come to me simply, with no sweet disguise.
With voice and lips and hands entune my heart
And wake the answering music in my eyes.

It often perturbs would-be poets to find that the urgency with which they try to capture the mood of the poem as it occurs to them, can lead to a loose interpretation of their idea. Worse than this is the worry that grammar, and correct structuring of language, is perhaps being sacrificed. Do not let these things worry you at this stage: the starting point is when only the essence of the poem is making itself audible. Words pouring out, and ideas of pattern, shape and form, are merely supporting a basic idea at this stage.

When struggling in this way, partly from a subconscious desire to develop the idea in conceptual form, it is the images that are important. The words coming to mind will be trying to make a pictorial relationship between the first instinct that motivated the poem and your understanding of that instinct. It may well be that the poem is nearly completed, at least in its first draft, before you arrive at such an understanding. It is usually only at this stage that you can begin to order language, and form.

What is happening is that details such as grammar are being put aside while in your own mind, you attempt to sort out new and possibly overwhelming perceptions about the reality of your subject matter.

Not all poets experience this, but those who do should not worry unduly about what appears to be a lack of logical thought. The poem will present itself eventually, as the structure becomes defined through any of the media chosen. At the outset it may appear to be a musical jumble of ideas, but once the original impression is recorded more selective work can begin.

The prime motivator, instinct, will be a guide. Once the idea for the poem is set down there will be time to correct grammar, order sentences, select words, and musical patterns. All of these, and others, will become vehicles for expressing thoughts and emotions.

Formal patterns are not the only methods with which to create a certain structure. An unusual method adopted by one poet is the use of dialogue, which links characters as well as the past and the present. Here is an example:

Cowslips by A.M. Sackett

'I remember
When I could sunfill my face

With fields of cowslips.'

Her eyes glazed
As she reflected her girlhood
And I longed to butter my chin
With the wild flowers of her youth.

Later that year
We took her to hidden country depths
And by the roadside
Full creamed and flourishing,

The cowslips bunched
On untouched banks.

'See, see,' she cried,
'That's how they used to be!'

The next example has a pictorial structure, which delicately defines the curves and shadows within a tiny shell.

Gift of a Snail Shell by A. Lewis-Smith

This shell is empty.
Light slides
into the first curve
then shadows spiral
to the hidden heart.

It is for you
to slip fantasies
within hollows.

Do not break it
for on first finding
I hid my dreams
deep in its dark
and they could shatter
with this shell.

The economy of words and line lengths concisely emphasises the theme of the poem. If read aloud slowly, the cadences of speech patterns can be heard and these emphasise the internal music of the poem.

We distribute cadences naturally, by the stresses in our patterns of speech, and are often guided by these as we write. A poem will sometimes dictate its form in this way, and by working to improve it by changing words, rhythm, rhyme and form, a correct and competent structure will be developed.

It has been shown in this chapter that the organisation of a poem does not have to follow a rigid pattern. What it should do is mould mood and emotion into an evocative whole, and the structure that is used should support this.

2
Untangled Thoughts

When a poet starts to write, an attempt is being made to capture the moment of inspiration. This may sound rather highflown, but it is what is happening nevertheless. It is essential that the way a poem presents itself is not ignored.

This may be in a few rhyming lines, or it may be in images. Possibly the form of the poem may present itself first, or a notion of the shape in which the poem is to be written may occur. It is rarely possible to coordinate the choice of any device we may use at this stage with the words that are coming to mind.

What happens first is a very instinctive process, and if it is possible to make notes of occurring thoughts, and to write the poem in rough outline, then do so. Thoughts and ideas will present themselves faster than they can be interpreted, and often the first way we put them into words will be tangled, illogical and ungrammatical. All of this can be put right when you begin the hard work of polishing the poem.

The excitement of writing poetry is the discovery of what is partially unknown about ourselves. A storm cloud may provoke a few descriptive lines, but as the writing progresses the cloud may prove to be the medium for something we had not anticipated. *North East* is a poem I started to write on a bitterly cold day, when even senses seemed cold, and the dull, grey light dominated everything. From the edge of a cliff it was noticeable how the wind had honed that edge over many years. It was a bleak area, and these thoughts influenced the poem as much as an inner meaning:

The wind
honed our fury
to spike-edged words,

trailing
on a breath of ice,
like frightened birds.

Shrouded,
the winter sun
eclipsed from us.

We screamed
our isolation
into that open place,

echoes
passed into
the silences of time,

the wind
snatching the
remnants of our dying.

Sometimes a poem will arrive with an image and will seem to follow a strict pattern, possibly a rhyming one. It is interesting that each poem arrives in a different way. My poem *North East* arrived from the stimulation of some visual effects, and through both external and internal influences.

A rhyming pattern can be predominant in the first stage of writing a poem, because the rhyme, used instinctively, moulds words into sentences and phrases. A rhyming pattern often helps our minds to achieve a swifter interpretation of the image, or the idea being presented.

This may be helpful during the initial stages of writing, when the poet sometimes feels bombarded by a clutter of ideas, words, and images. Rather than lose the mood of the poem it is best to let the rhyme define the meaning, and to lay direct emphasis on relevant details in the poem. During the revision stage the rhyming pattern can be changed or even omitted entirely. If a rhyming pattern is strategically placed, it may help to record ideas, and it may help if an alphabet rhyming pattern is followed (there are many patterns, discussed in chapter ten). These guides are one way of defining a rhyme, so that the one finally chosen can be adhered to throughout the poem. Here are two examples in which we set out alphabet rhyming patterns:

And were the world to end today A
We must all kneel down and pray A
Hope is now our guiding star B
Dreams are spent and flung afar B

If I find love is a better way A
And this one thing needed throughout time *B*
I'll pursue it, and find it in each day A
Then lock it in music, and my rhyme B

Rhymes made this way result from the repetition at the end of a number of lines. Rhymes may be made on alternating or consecutive lines, and variations on rhymes can be made at the poet's discretion.

If the poem is read aloud when it is nearing completion, the importance of the rhyme will be heard. Try to read your poems to a group of people, possibly fellow poets whom you respect. Make a point of not reading your work to relatives and close friends, you will not get an unbiased criticism this way. You will more than likely be told 'it is very nice', or that they 'understand it'. What you require at this point is either to rely upon your own judgement or, if you are uncertain, to seek comment and constructive criticism from fellow writers.

If a rhyming pattern is decided upon as the best medium, and the one you have chosen is not purely doggerel but serves the poem well, then keep to that particular pattern.

Put the poem away for a while, then bring it out again after a week or two, and ask yourself the three questions:

1: Is the rhyme retained in a regular pattern throughout the poem?

2: Has the rhyming pattern been changed abruptly from stanza to stanza?

3: Are the rhymes too contrived as for instance in:

a man in love
looks at the moon above

The following poem, *Intrusions*, illustrates how a poem that arrived following a strict adherence to rhyme began to lose the impetus that made the poet write it. The rhymes, although in the first stage of the poem's development rather contrived, had helped him retain the original thought. Rhyming patterns help the flow of ideas and language.

At a poetry workshop the writer was helped with the reworking of his poem. He had already decided that a rhyming pattern was not necessary to project his predominant theme – the sense of being trapped, and that some things are beyond personal control. Here are the two versions of the poem:

Intrusions (First draft) by J.M. Sharman
Last night, as I lay fast asleep,
We had some snow, not very deep.
It melted in the morning sun
And all had gone by half-past one.

The night before, I woke from sleep
To bleating of a cornered sheep.
She bleated till the break of day
Till someone helped her get away.

This afternoon some jets flew by,
Shattering the silence of the sky.
Once, twice, three times they passed, and then
The countryside was quiet again.

By stealth, persistence, force,
Life is diverted from its course.

In trying to put some form round the idea that came to him, and in attempting to make a concise statement, the poet used a rhyming pattern of: a a b b. He recognised that some of the rhymes were contrived, and through revision he deliberately set out to lose them. The workshop he attended agreed with this: the rhymes had started as a way of structuring his thoughts, but had ended by inhibiting his attempt to convey his meaning and mood. After much hard work, the poem finished like this:

The other night I was woken
by a cornered sheep, bleating.
Trapped too,
I dressed and released her,
so we could both sleep.

The snow last night
did not wake me,
but I felt resentful
that evening-green had turned dawn-white
unheralded.

This afternoon two jets
cut the calm of nature,
once, twice, three times; then
nature was restored,
and I had forgotten my thoughts.

By persistence, stealth or force,
preconceived life is always
being diverted.

The rhyme had served a useful purpose at first, but losing its restrictions allowed the poem to unfold its theme more effectively. The conciseness the poet felt necessary for the style of the poem is helped where enjambment is used – this is the running on the sense of one stanza line to the next without pause (note this in the second and third stanzas).

If the vitality goes from a poem, it is often because our

thoughts are not being streamed into coherent patterns. Subconsciously, we hold on to whatever special effects propel our thoughts along, such as instinctive speech patterns which seem to define a rhythm or rhyme. Rhyming patterns have to be very well selected, or they can limit our interpretation of the meaning of a poem, and produce images that are not suited to the context.

The natural rhythms of speech can initially direct the format of a poem, but the poet has to untangle thoughts by controlling such rhythms. The English language, if spoken correctly, has rhythms which vary accordingly to the way words are arranged. Stressed and unstressed syllables give variety to speech, and music to poetry. In ordinary speech the stresses come at irregular intervals. Look at a few examples:

I feel you will
I hope all is well
I will think of you tonight
I am sure I said that this matter was urgent

These examples could have been snippets of conversation overheard in a shop, on a bus, or in a restaurant. Note the stresses, and the rise and fall of the pattern making a natural flow of rhythm. This is how a poem is often quite instinctively directed, and it is often the rhythm in the selected words that influence the pattern and form of a poem.

As you write your poetry, take time to read the words aloud. You will often be able to hear if any stresses of speech produce a jarring effect. You can also decide how to use the stress patterns to emphasise the atmosphere and meaning of the poem.

When revising, the methods that have been used quite instinctively can be examined and changed if necessary. We apply instinct and the heart to begin with, then use logic and more restrained thought as the poem progresses.

Sometimes when composing, the original idea is not carried along in any set pattern. The words that arise from the first thoughts about a poem, often merely follow the natural speech cadences. If the whole poem arrives rapidly, it will sometimes have a rhyme at the end that thumps out its message or meaning. We all work in different ways, and this often is one way that the mind records the idea propelling it along. After this, it is then necessary to deliberate over what devices will emphasise the main points of the poem.

In a poem called *Timespan* I began as follows:

In warm sun-strident afternoons
I followed my father
under the sloping roof
of greenhouse glass,

and stood beside him
smelling the ripening green
and flanked by pots
that held mysteries, he'd planted, watered – watched.

This is how the poem first arrived, with a small, insistent, echoing rhyme, which at first was placed at the end of the poem. However, another stanza followed, and this heralded a patterning of vowels:

We did not speak; at his side
I stood sure and unafraid, while sunlight
spread through diadems of days,
as gentle-fingered he firmed a root, or reaching up
beyond his head, felt in the vine for globuled fruit.

The positioning of the words *unafraid* and *days* made a further echo, while the words *root* and *fruit*, and others in the stanzas that followed, brought a continuity to the echo pattern. Another stanza, coming to mind in a rush, proved to be the final one:

Now, as my hands loosen earth
with trowel and fork,
I savour memories,
and seed mysteries in terracotta pots.

An approximate rhyme can create a musical effect. A rhyme deliberately created in this way can often involve changing the vowel or the consonants. For example instead of *man* and *ban* which rhyme and chime exactly, the words *sun* and *man* would be used to create a slant rhyme pattern. It is most often the vowels that are changed.

There is an echo of the rhyme in the middle of *Timespan*, created by the words *pots* and *watched*. The poem became longer than had first been anticipated, and the completed version is as follows:

Timespan

In warm,
sun-strident afternoons
I followed my father to his sanctuary,
beneath the sloping roof
of greenhouse glass,

and stood beside him
cloistered in quietness,
smelling the ripening green, and flanked
by pots that held mysteries
he'd planted, watered – watched.

We did not speak; at his side
I stood sure and unafraid, while sunlight
spread through diadems of days,
as gentle-fingered he firmed a root, or reaching up
beyond his head, felt in the vine for globuled fruit.

Now, as my hands loosen earth
with trowel and fork,
I savour memories, excavating roots,
and seeding mysteries
in terra cotta pots.

The pattern which has been formed through the slant and echo rhymes can be noted.

When we begin to formulate the poem that is in our minds,

and jot down those first few words, we may find we have used sentences that are clichéd, rhymes that are doggerel, and images that are unwieldy. These can all be improved when a pattern is formed that is suitable for the poem.

If a poem seems at first to follow no particular pattern, then the basic idea just written out in a few lines, rather like a block of prose, should be broken down into the steady beat and thrust of rhythmic speech patterns. Linking words that echo, as the example given in *Timespan*, can be an effective way to progress.

The line, as opposed to the sentence, is a poet's musical score – or it can be if used properly. A metrical pattern can be applied to each line either when composing, or when revising the poem (see chapter four for metrical patterns). Here is an exercise for you to try:

> Attempt to write a poem in short lines merely following natural cadences of speech, using the beats of stressed and unstressed syllables within the line.
>
> Note if alliteration, which is the occurrence of the same letter or sound at the beginning of several words, and/or assonance which is the resemblance of sound between syllables appear in the lines, and note if they help the basic idea of the poem.
>
> Develop throughout the poem any half rhymes or full rhymes, so that a sequence of these is formed.

Rhyme, rhythm, and imagery seem to be the devices used most instinctively when writing poetry. Alliteration, which is explained above, seems to be easily triggered off by memory. There is nothing wrong with this, providing such a device is well chosen to illustrate relevant and major points in a poem. It is not enough to allow our memory simply to produce well worn phrases to order. *Sing a Song of Sixpence*, easily recognisable as an alliterative line from infant days, would presumably not slip into one of our poems, but repetitive sounds might easily emerge in a line of a poem such as: *She sat on the sixth step waiting*... But the continuing use of alliteration could project the image of this woman as: *and the ghostlike greyness...*

A stanza is being evolved this way, and the language used is helping to control the idea. It requires careful analysis of each line as the poem develops, to ensure that the pattern of alliteration defines exactly what the poet intends. For instance, does *ghostlike greyness* achieve anything at all? It does bring perhaps a sense of atmosphere within a line of poetry, but if the next line is *tombstones emerge through mist...* the poem is being merely descriptive. It has to be asked at this point therefore: Is this enough? Would the image and atmosphere be better defined by using another device as well as that of alliteration? For example, *Tall tombstones, like fingers of fear...* would add to image and atmosphere by alliteration plus simile.

When working on alliteration be wary of placing more than three alliterative words together. In, for example, *heard him hurrying* we have suitable alliterative words that illustrate something; but move to *heard him hurrying home* and it all begins to resemble a tongue twisting exercise.

Here is another exercise you might try:

> Select several words that form an alliterative pattern suitable for the poem being worked on. These words can be nouns, adjectives or verbs.
>
> Use three of the words chosen in one line of a poem for instance: sunset slipped sky
>
> Then extend the poem so that the words chosen are on different lines.
>
> As in:- The rays of a sunset
> slipped from view
> in a mottled, cloudy sky.

This exercise shows how to group individual sounds for artistic effect. It is a natural tendency to mass certain sounds together. It is still necessary when revising, however, to check that the sound patterns selected, are the best ones for the poem.

A bad example would be: *The sun's rays reached rose red round Ruston Bridge.* It can be heard when reading this line aloud that the construction of consonantal and alliterative sounds merely creates a stumbling block for the reader. The alliterative use of the letter *r* has been overused, and the hard sounding letter *d* breaks up any musical flow that may have been developing.

By use of alliteration, assonance, repetitive sounds, echoing rhymes, and speech patterns, the poet can skilfully lead readers through a poem.

Certain patterns can be used quite instinctively when untangling thoughts during the writing process. Assonance for instance, which is the repetition of the same vowel sounds: it is worth asking yourself every so often when writing whether a particular vowel echo would add strength to a poem.

Alliteration has a quality that makes it stick in the memory, but the repetition of initial consonants can be varied. The alliterative sound can be produced by a combination as well as a single letter, as for example in the words *grim*, *grain* and *gross*.

It may be found helpful when working on a poem to underline or put inverted commas around words that provide assonance or alliteration. If these are checked in more detail later, you may find a pattern of sound being followed through them. This pattern might emerge as the basis of a form that suits the theme of your poem.

Patterns of rhyme can be formed through assonantal and consonantal sounds as in *lash* and *wash*, or *pattern* and *fatter*.

As an exercise write a few words of a poem and underline the stressed and unstressed syllables as well as the vowels and consonants. Try to complete a stanza where the syllables are regularly stressed in each line. Then take either the vowels or the consonants and also keep to a regular pattern of these in the lines.

Our senses are the faculties for receiving sensations, and carefully chosen sound patterns can echo such sensations. It is possible, as you become more experienced in the craft of writing poetry, to choose certain devices deliberately. These must be used subtly to avoid any appearance of contrivance.

If, when revising a poem, it is found to contain a pattern of echoes that has formed through any instinctive pattern (often a vowel or consonant pattern) then try to maintain this sequence throughout the poem.

It is not an easy task, but it will help you to disentangle the primary thought that brought the poem into existence. In other words it will coordinate your thoughts. It is always a good idea when writing a poem to periodically ask yourself the following questions.

1: Is the main idea conveyed throughout the poem?
2: Is the poem too obscure?
3: Would a deliberate pattern of rhyme, alliteration or assonance improve the poem?

An image can encompass the entire meaning of a poem, especially as it first springs to mind through speech patterns, alliteration, rhymes and other instinctive ways. However, this first image may well prove to be too dominant for the poem. It may be that the poem should have a gentle pace, a quiet melodious voice, and the image transferred in the intense heat of recording the poem may be altogether too strident. For example:

blood red juice of cherries
trickled down her mouth...

would bring a vampirish vision to mind, when possibly the poem is intended to be about a small and delicate child, and not part of the undead scenario!

All this can be checked when the poem is revised. It is important to remember that, up to this point, the poem (or its essence) is merely being recorded. Now the poet has to direct the essence, or the impulse as I called it previously, and marshal words, images, and patterns, into some sort of order.

It is obvious from the example given that what the poet was transcribing was a picture of someone eating cherries. This image it can be assumed is highly relevant to the poem, and therefore, the poet was right to capture it quickly. Only during the revision process can a more logical use of words with which to surround the image be considered. At this time, the poet (again in this case a student) proceeds to order her thoughts:

I saw her smile,
watched her bite the blood red cherries
juice stained her tiny teeth,
Julie aged five.

The smile is now relevant to the poem, and we are told there is a child involved in the story. The next logical progression led to this:

Watching her, the unease slipped away,
Julie was well again.

The logic in the progression was the unfolding explanation that the child in the poem had been unwell. The smile referred to is very necessary because it relates to the child having been unwell, but now being well and joyful. The vigour of the bite on that cherry needs to be emphasised to show she is full of strength, but not expressed in the original vampirish image. Continual revision brought the poem to its conclusion:

Watching her, the unease slipped away,
Julie was well again
the moulded limbs of childhood firm.

I saw her smile
watched her small teeth imprint
the cherry with her hard bite,

watched the cherry juice
trickle down her mouth, watched her
toss her head, and laugh, rejoicing,
Julie aged five.

The poem developed from the first idea, and that too-strident image, and the words *her small teeth imprint* and *hard bite* relate to the child's new found fitness. The poet not only untangled thoughts, but also began to structure the poem through certain rhythms relating to consonants and through such small things as the well chosen repetition of *watched*.

This poem started with an image, and was developed and improved by the structure which evolved through the effective use of sound patterns, as in wat*ch*ed/*ch*ildhood/*ch*erry, and in the slight echo in the words *laugh* and *five*, as well as *again* and *firm*. Order has been brought to what at first appeared somewhat chaotic lines with a too dominant image.

Simile and metaphor are two excellent ways of developing imagery, simile being an explicit likening of one thing to another, often using the words *like* and *as*:

> *The girls in bright dresses, danced across the grass like butterflies.*

Metaphor is a comparison between two objects not usually thought to have anything in common, as in a malicious woman being called 'a spiteful cat'. Here is a set of exercises that will be useful at this stage:

EXERCISES FOR SIMILE AND METAPHOR

1: Describe a scene or character that gives plenty of opportunity to establish likenesses.
2: Make a list of trees, animals, birds, and compare each of them with something else, using the words *as* or *like*.
3: Write a series of lines that begin:

> *The moon is...*
> *The sky is...*
> *My house is...*

Complete each line with a word that describes the object, but strive for originality. You might write for example: The moon is a silver wheel (or as a child, who was describing a crescent moon wrote: The moon is a banana).

EXERCISES FOR IMAGERY

1: Coordinate thoughts by writing a title for a poem that is in itself an image. Extend this into a poem.
2: Reconstruct an incident from memory, using concrete, specific words.
3: Describe a daylight scene, then a night-time one. Use metaphor at least once in each description.
4: Describe in two lines how something tasted (for instance, an unripe apple).
5: Write a stanza describing something heard (for instance, waves beating against rocks).

If an image is first contained in a few lines of a poem, by extending the image into other stanzas, the poem can be unravelled, and organised. For instance if the first solitary image that came to mind was of birds, and this description placed baldly as the opening line:

Sparrows on a line

then the possible extension of that line could be:

Sparrows on a line like notes of music
black against blue
they sit, silent

Here the connotation of ideas lead to other lines and a second image follows in the second and third lines:

tails up, beaks out
form black dots,
quavers on thin stretched marks.

Remember that the magic is retained in a poem by the use of an original image, as well as an original line or word. Structures and devices have to be used with sensitivity and delicacy so that the reader is unaware that the magic is enhanced by their use. Take a look in museums and libraries, at any manuscripts of those numbered amongst our greatest poets. Wordsworth, Tennyson, Byron, Shelley, Keats, and many others, all captured that elusive magic and secured it within the confines of words. They worked like sculptors, chiselling and paring down images. They formed patterns and pictures in their poems, retaining the essential quality within deliberate structures.

When writing a poem we are revealing something – both to ourselves, for we sometimes view reality in a different way when composing, and to those who will eventually read the poem. Sound patterns, including those mentioned in this chapter, help to structure the idea, scene, emotion, or perhaps a character, that is being presented. Try not to work when overtired. Leave the first draft for at least a few days. The first impulse that started the poem is just a preliminary sketch.

When a poem is nearing completion, then it is time to ask whether the essential quality, the essence of it, has been defined and untangled by a logical thought process.

3
LETTING GO

The imagination, where all senses combine to illustrate certain ideas, is allowed full rein when writing poetry. The imagination can be inhibited, however, while the poet works on the technical points that hopefully will improve a poem. It cannot be emphasised enough that the poem must first be allowed to develop in its own way. If the rush of words, ideas and phrases come in a disorganised fashion, this should be allowed to happen. If the first strength of the imagination delivers a whole concept, then this should be recorded quickly, the muddled way it arrives can be improved later.

Ideally, to allow the imagination to predominate for long periods, one would have to live in a state of perpetually heightened awareness. It is not, of course, possible to maintain such a state of mind. One can however recognise when the imagination is being stimulated, and can experience heightened powers of perception at such times.

In the fast pace of life it is easy to believe that we experience the world primarily through our eyes. By concentrating, particularly when our powers of perception are heightened, we can bring our other senses into play and our heightened awareness will stimulate the imagination and our ideas can be recorded into poems.

Emotions can, for example, be triggered off, through our sense of hearing. It is a well known fact that the sound of a ship's fog horn evokes feelings of a lonely, haunting quality. Think of other sounds, and the emotions that they produce in us. A child's sob, the hoot of an owl, the hiss of car windscreen wipers, the regular loud ticking of a clock, or the hammered, steady beat of a pile driver in action. Placing each of these sounds in a given situation can produce the ingredients necessary for a poem.

For example, if the imaginary pile driver is on the bank of a river, where there had been several, small pretty cottages well known to us, and where someone well known to us had lived, it would come as a shock to realise that these buildings are now demolished.

Let us take this imaginary situation one step further: a promenade is being built where once the cottages stood, and the pile driver is banging in steel supports for it. The essence of a poem that might come to mind is the idea that what had once been familiar no longer exists. The heavy hammering of the pile driver emphasises the harshness of the reality. This sound could become the impetus for a poem and should be reproduced perhaps by use of alliteration, strict metrical beat, syllable count, or perhaps by the repetition of certain words or phrases:

The path vibrates with noise,
dispirited I watch the men at work
and hear the constant
smash and thump
smash and thump

the rise and fall of consistent noise.

The cottages have gone, demolished
beneath the same sound,
smash and thump
smash and thump

of pile driver, pick, and shovel...

Now try some exercises

Exercise 1: The sobbing child is in a doctor's waiting room. Let your imagination conjure up something from this scene, try to use the supportive structure that emphasises the emotion within such a scene. Choose language carefully to convey atmosphere.

Exercise 2: Imagine that it is night time: the moon is hidden by clouds, and you are in a dense woodland area; various sounds are frightening, mysterious, or reassuring. Describe these, then assemble them in a poem, using descriptive language and metaphor to highlight your feelings about this situation.

There are other senses we can draw on that will help in the letting go process and these are visual, olfactory, tactile, kinetic and gustatory.

Memory combined with imagination can bring a poem to mind. For instance, using the sense of smell (olfactory), a poem describing a garden may develop from the memory of a bonfire, the bonfire may be the reminder of childhood, and the poem could have a nostalgic touch.

A very visual poem instigated by the sense of sight is *Monet's Garden* by S. Skinner.

Summer at Giverny, red fish swim
in a reflected garden, flower and fern
their speckled heaven; flick a downward path
through shades of green to dark hypnotic depths
that mingle earth and sky and may alert
the drowning upside down world of the heart.

Paintings draw us to those depths, return
us to this quiet room in the museum
where Monet puts his finger on the soul.
Winds scallop water, willows trail,
long shadows graze, a wild hedge
of colour overgrows the painter's bridge.

They say he was becoming blind: his sunlights
spray like surf on leaves, burnish the white
lilies in his pool. Impressions float
easily and yet his vision sets
a stillness on the rainbow sun and makes
a beauty of all things that flower and break.

As an exercise, try to write a poem about a certain scene that impresses you, but if the scene also reminds you of some incident from childhood, then this memory should also be placed within the poem.

There are conflicting viewpoints amongst poets as to whether memories should be omitted from a poem, and whether only the imagination should dominate. The idea behind such reasoning is that, by applying purely imaginative ideas, the language chosen to define them will be innovative.

Memory, however, often encroaches on imaginative thought, especially when it is stimulated by something enveloping our senses.

The audio example given earlier in this chapter, typifies how the imagination can induce our minds to let go and swing into a reflective mood. Consequently, certain memories related to the particular sense that instigated the imaginative thought will intrude. Perhaps intrude is not the correct word to use. For memories, motivated by a particular sense, can be excellent allies when writing poetry. They convey a mood or emotion, and it is the sense of these that the poet strives to interpret and place in a poem.

Gustatory sense, that of taste, can be strong enough to induce an image, and this image will bring the start of our poem to us. Perhaps the image is of someone eating an apple. We can apply our imagination as to how this is done. The image coming to mind could be that of a young woman, she is dressed casually in jeans and sweatshirt, she is eating an apple as she walks through an orchard. We might describe her as *munching* an apple. Why *munching*, and not simply *biting* an apple? Because to munch something, is to chew it with a marked action of the jaws, this would be a steady, deliberate action. The word munching sets off connotations. She also walks in a steady, and deliberate way. She strolls, and does not stride along the orchard. The poem develops in the following way, and is called *The Meeting*:

She strolled
through long feathered grass,
sunlight flicked through leaves
and boughs, and ripe apples weighed them down.

Munching, she crisped the fruit
between sharp teeth, relishing the taste,
sunlight warmed her head, and the white sweat-shirt
was tightly tucked into her jeans;
she glimpsed the tall figure of a man
who ran the intervening space between them,
calling her name.

She slowed her pace, and nonchalantly
tossed the apple core among dropped leaves
and blossom on the ground.
Turning slowly towards the eager man,
she inclined her head

but merely offered him a half-smile.

The whole attitude of the woman in the poem is casual, induced by the connotations of the word *munching*. Her dress, manner of walking, even the way she eats the apple, are all casual. The man however, is eager and he runs the space between them, and calls to her, while she, nonchalantly tosses the apple core aside; a deliberate action, done before she turns to acknowledge him with a slight half smile. The whole of this description has been developed from imagination, but it may well have been a memory of the taste of a ripe apple that enabled the imagination of the poet to let go and attempt to write the poem.

Exercise: In a few lines describe the taste of something:
a) bitter b) sweet c) salty

Put one of these descriptions into the first or last stanza of a poem, introduce a character in the poem, male or female, young or old.

A proportion of the poem that you write, perhaps most of it, will be devised through the medium of the imagination. Memory too, however, will play its part in bringing your ideas to light. Make a mental note of how much of the poem relies on memory.

Exercise: Try to recall an incident that brings to mind sensations of amazement, apprehension, fear, happiness. Try linking one of these sensations with a description of either the place, or imagined place where the sensation occurred. Develop the description further and develop also the emotive factor into a poem.

It is important to take note of small things, the way clouds move over the moon, how someone's expression changes when they speak, how a leaf flutters down from a bush or tree (which incidentally is the kinetic sense). The power of the senses discussed in this chapter are always with us; if we ignore them, or the way they can be used to help in the writing of poetry, then we lose something valuable.

The idea that a poet sits in the garret to write poetry is not strictly true. A poet probably has his or her own idea of what this garret consists of. It may be somewhere that is conducive to writing. The garret may simply be an area in a poet's mind, where the poem in hand is worked on. Many poets today are involved in work of varying descriptions: teachers, carpenters, cooks, gardeners, to name a few. It is not necessary to live the life of a recluse to write poetry, although this may be a necessary part of being a poet to some. What is necessary is that perceptions should be continually sharpened, so that even familiar objects can be seen in a different way. A child of nine, taking part in a school poetry workshop, impressed me by thinking up the whole concept for a poem and describing an image in three lines:

Night is a black drape
that curtains the sky with stars
moonlight a white silky skin

This familiar scene described in such a way, takes on a significant beauty.

Exercise: Examine a familiar object closely, it can be something in the home, garden, or at work. Describe this object in a way that makes it sound extraordinary.

Example: Daisies, like delicate embroidery are scattered on the lawn.

Exercise: Use the description you first thought of in a poem, either place it in the first stanza, or the last, or turn it into a refrain.

The language used in poetry has several functions. The main ones are to express ourselves, and to communicate our thoughts to others. By learning to let go, and keeping our perceptions sharp, it is possible to find new ways with which to define the ordinary. These have to be understood by readers however. It is not wrong to write obscure poetry, but there is a definite feeling of reward when it is obvious that a reader, or listener, becomes fully aware of the implied meaning within a poem. Emotions should not be portrayed too dominantly within lines, and poets should learn how to restrain them. An example below shows how the poet, by careful selection of words, enhances emotive quality without too stridently declaring it. The words *pilgrimage* and *keening* achieve this, and the suggestion of a *draped shadow* brings the final powerful image in this extract from the poem *Family Photographs* by P. Carradice:

There is no picture
to denote your passing.

But Laugharne, some weeks before –
'We always go', you said. 'Our pilgrimage.'
And so we drove
and high above the Boathouse, rested.
I pointed, clicked my camera
as you sat, half lay within the car.
Later, after death,
developed prints fell, keening,
through the door. The car was perfect
but your body, draped by shadow,
was obscured.
As if you never were.

Emotions can be emphasised by the pace of a poem. The example below shows how the device known as enjambment, where one line flows onto the next without pause, creates a fast pace and is used to emphasise the flight of birds and joyous emotive quality of the whole poem:

Today, the sun is gold and bright
the birds are on the wing
and all is filled with such delight
the very air doth sing!

(The rhyme also helps create a fast pace.) To highlight meaning or atmosphere, repetitive words can be used:

Cloud heaped on cloud
black cloud,
and rain, rain that continued
into the black night...

Dialogue, a conversation carried on through lines of poetry, will often describe characters or the meaning deep within a poem. An example is *Prawle Point*:

Water, like pewter, silver dull
reflects a dour month – March, and rain slants
needle-wise into our faces so that we gasp
toiling up Prawle Point, through lanes wreathed
with blackthorn's Easter blossoming.

Sheep stare at our approach then move
to higher paths, primroses still bloom, and I recall
last year you said,
'they look like clumps of scattered sun.'

It was easier then, matching my step to your stride.
I miss you,
miss sheltering under sea-smooth rocks
miss your body shielding mine against the gale's thrust.

The others understand my sudden silences,
call across areas of red earth
the wind bringing only their endings
'not far,
keep going...'

At the highest point waves back up
against tooth-edged rocks, the cliffs vibrate with them,
and sea-spray like tears, tastes salt in my memory.

There is a certain danger in the sense of letting go which poets have to avoid: any device can be overworked and the poem can lose its first impetus. Repetition would be irksome if used too much, and a poem would consequently become boring. Variation is required between lines and words to avoid this.

Opinions and attitudes are reflected in the way language is used. If a poet is not careful when airing a personal viewpoint the poem develops as a lecture, and the poet is seen as a lecturer, rather than as a poet. The voice of the poet can intrude through a too judgmental viewpoint, often where open statement dominates the poem. This should be checked during the process of examination and revision.

Subtle ways of strengthening a statement can be used. Direct imagery is one method, where the image illustrates a statement but does not convey the overall meaning. Repetition again, or a strong metrical beat, places emphasis on statements also, and rhyme is one way to add emphasis that poets over the years have found effective.

Didactic poetry, where the poet deliberately sets out to convey a message, has to be well controlled; language, structure and form require careful scrutiny (an example of such poetry is Milton's *Paradise Lost*). This does not mean that controversial issues have to be avoided. Poems relating to a particular background and culture are of interest to society as a whole. Sensitivity and sensibility combined will help when writing didactic or statement-like poetry.

A tendency to intrude has to be overcome when first letting go. The poet's voice should not be too obvious. How can one avoid this? It is possible to detect where a poet has lectured, or been too subjective, or judgmental in viewpoint when there is an overuse of subjective tones, literal images, or strident repetitions of certain phrases. Rhythms, vowel patterns, intense rhyming sequences, or overuse of a strict metrical beat are also often used as mediums to enforce a personal message. If these are used too much, however, they will detract from a poem's true worth. Try to limit the use of such devices without withholding any vital statement necessary to convey the theme of the poem.

Mere statement of course does not make good poetry. Challenging as it is, try to keep some music, or metaphor within the poem of statement; these will differentiate it from the statement of prose.

The aim of any form or technique used in poetry is to make poems appear to have developed naturally. Whatever methods are chosen to enhance a poem, or to deliver its message, these should be used discreetly. This of course includes making a statement about something or someone. A poem that makes a statement should not be presented in a direct manner, as in prose, but with the obvious merely implied and the statement conveyed by subtle methods.

A poet learns through experience how to control various mediums of expression. Letting go of subjective thought patterns and analysing one's own work enables the poet to change style, form, and even direction of a poem.

A method of expression often evolves from an image, and if this is accompanied by a certain rhythm a good style can develop. If the rhythm seems to be lacking in vitality the image can be retained by embodying it within a repetitive line, from this the poem may develop its own rhythm and chant. Chanting is an ancient rhythm often associated with church music and with the ritualistic singing of witches and magicians:

Turn the earth,
Turn the earth,
Over and over,
Sink spade in clay
Lift the sweet clover.

Turn the earth,
Turn the earth
Drop in the seeds,
Bend the back down
Lift out the weeds.

Turn the earth,
Turn the earth
Under the sun,
Heat and rain nourish
The wheat that will come.

Turn the earth,
Turn the earth
Harvest has come,
Lift the good food
All to take home.

When no idea springs to mind for a poem, and the idea, form and pattern are elusive, then go back to the senses – those discussed earlier in this chapter. This may help in the process of letting go. For instance the sense of touch can bring an association of ideas. Try grasping a cold pebble, this coldness can relate to other senses. It can bring reminders of winter if you try to describe the coldness, and here memory will play its part again. These associated ideas can be the basis of a poem.

The smoothness of the pebble can release other associated ideas: it might for example suggest jewellery. For the purpose of this exercise in letting go, let us take a pearl as the jewel, which hopefully will set off connections for other images and ideas for a poem.

A pearl can be a raindrop, or a tear in the eyes of a child. Pearl also relates to the sheen of skin, or the pearl lustre of a finger nail. The mind will cooperate in our search for related images. The next struggle is to avoid the use of clichés, for instance *raindrops like pearls*. Perhaps the *glisten of pearled raindrops* might be a better image? By concentrating, connections of images can be brought to mind. Some exercises:

Exercise 1: Use the image of the stone, or the pearl, or ice, or a suitable connection that occurs, and place it in the stanza of a poem, having first combined the image with a description of a room, a garden, a tree, a person.
Try over a period of time to extend the poem, use the image first thought of as the crux of the poem.

Exercise 2: Select any object, and write ten to fourteen lines of a poem introducing this object. Try to stretch your powers of imagination, and allow memories to aid you.

Having described your chosen object in some way, try to establish what pattern best suits the poem. If for example the poem is about a stone, consider if it was once on a beach with the sea lapping at it. Fit the rhythm of waves, long syllabled words perhaps, or use lines with short choppy rhymes to illustrate small waves. You may feel that descriptive use of language and a metrical pattern would suit your idea best. If you write the poem in sonnet form, try to use clearly defined images. The rhythmic chant pattern may be best suited for your story. Experiment, try different rhyming schemes.

Line lengths can be made anywhere that the poet thinks appropriate to the subject, and this may help in the letting go process. The poet breaks the line where necessary for shock purposes, or simply to tell the reader to take a pause, or to create suspense and tension.

In the following stanza taken from one of my old notebooks, the sentences can be seen to be broken at line endings. By the use of punctuation within the lines however, readers are shown where to pause. The pace of the poem is clearly defined in this way:

... neat stooks of rifles, tents, and men who moved
like shadows, passing beneath the window
of my room, carrying accoutrements of war
while I, unobserved, watched the steady to and fro
until a whistle shrilled, and they ran
doubled up in rows.

By paying attention to vowels and consonants, a line can be made rhythmic. Stressed and unstressed syllables can be noted and marked if a rhythmic pattern seems to be maturing as the poem progresses. Sometimes freedom from metrical patterns can bring spontaneity to the writing process. If a poem has been written in a free verse way, check to see whether the cadences in speech patterns enhance the poem when it is read aloud. A rhythmic quality can be achieved by using hard sounding consonants in cooperation with the rise and fall in speech patterns. Vowels, too, if used in long and short sounds (as for instance in the words *blow* and *boom* or *room* and *rose*) can create a pattern, particularly if used in the same lines in each stanza.

Once a theme has come to mind, and the poem is being written, then each stanza can hold a new idea surrounding the theme. Occasionally a line comes to mind that appears quite obviously to be the first line for a poem. Write it down as the first line, but do not be surprised to find this line is moved to another position as you progress.

Sometimes a single word comes to mind. It might be a word that fascinates you by the way it sounds. 'Elongate' was a word that persisted in my mind until eventually I used it in a poem. Write down a list of such words and keep them handy. One of these may be the very word you need to use as a symbol, or to include in a line of repetition, or even to create a more musical effect.

Sometimes it is the title for a poem that comes to mind first, and the connotations of the title can bring fresh ideas. Rhymes too, often have a way of carrying a thought process along. This thought may be related to an image, or sense, or emotion. It can also be an idea of a place or a person.

The rhyming sequence most favoured when trying to convey thoughts rapidly, is where rhymes occur on line-endings, usually alternate ones. This is a good way to record thoughts, but in its strict form may be limiting in the exercise of letting go. Rhymes can be made to occur at more irregular intervals, possibly in the middle of lines, or simply at the end of a poem as a way of drawing the whole thing together.

Rhyming couplets, formed by two successive lines of

poetry that rhyme, can help the thought process by retaining it within this tight sequence. The development of ideas can extend from the original two lines if necessary, and the poem can be made into a longer version.

A rhyming pattern that originated in the 16th century, but is rarely used now, is the echo rhyme. The poem can be written following a simple but strict design of one long line and an answering one-word rhyme:

echo
Through vistas of wide and leafy archways green
seen
As beatitudes from heaven, glimpsed by my eye
why?
Wisdom of solitude, natural delights of earth
mirth
Bird's song, joy of sunshine, colours and sky
die
When confined in city noise, and grime and sights
nights
Encompassing the lonely time, unknown faces, fears
tears
Now, in this green heaven all find the quiet place
peace

It should not be assumed that poetry can be created by technicalities: if effects and devices are too contrived they can inhibit the flow of good poetry. The suggested ideas, and exercises given in this chapter will hopefully persuade beginners and others that, by attempting to let go and trying different modes of expression, a freshness of approach can be brought to their work.

4
Music In The Air

The music in a poem can be haunting, thumping, quiet or loud. It can produce a chant, lullaby or song, whatever the poet requires.

It is obvious from hearing poems read aloud, and yet sometimes forgotten, that poetry is meant to be heard as well as read, and that a rhyming pattern will produce its own music. Rhyme is made from a variety of repetitive sounds, and these are discussed in another chapter. It follows therefore, that alliteration is a sort of rhyme. Alliteration is used for artistic effect, and is made by repetition of individual consonant sounds.

Too much alliteration at the beginning of words can change a poem into something resembling a tongue twisting, and often humorous, piece of work. Take for example: *Surely sixty songs sung sincerely seem suitable?*

It is obvious that poets should avoid such excessive use of this device. If, however, alliteration is used in a sensible way, it does set up a rhythmic quality that appears to flow like music:

The soft silk flows smoothly round her thighs.

When the consonants are not placed at the beginning of words, but used alliteratively within lines, the sounds are used in what is known as a consonantal device.

Assonance can be used to achieve similar musical effects. This is created by the repetitive use of vowel sounds, and these produce certain echoes within the structure of lines:

It came swiftly, silently, like a fallen cloud

drifting snow over the hills

There are a number of vowel sounds within these two lines (other than those that are marked), but those marked produce a lingering, echoing effect. Another choice would be for the poet to concentrate solely on two distinctive sounds, perhaps the *i* as in *it* and *swiftly*. If the vowels are marshalled in a certain grouping, a musical effect is created and a type of melody is made.

If patterns of vowels and consonants are retained throughout stanzas, the musical quality of a poem will be improved. This obviously requires very careful consideration of the words chosen within lines and groupings. A difficult feat, but one that is rewarding when achieved.

Alliteration, assonance and repetition all create music by helping to establish rhythm, and rhythm is an active power, reinforcing the content of a poem. It sounds, when describing these techniques, that they are merely used by poets as mechanical devices. It is true that poets have to consider where to place such aids, but it is equally important to understand why they are used.

It will be found very helpful to read as much as possible of the work of major poets. Both traditional and contemporary poetry makes use of technical aids. Once aware of where certain devices have been placed in poems it will be seen how much of these, if used skilfully, can enrich them.

Consonants and vowels assist in the development of the musical structure of a poem, while repetition of complete words can form a pattern of notes. A poem where some vital word appears at set intervals can create a regularity that is musical in its effect.

An example of this can be seen in Tennyson's poem, *The Lady of Shalott*, where an array of images and flights of language balances the constant repetition of certain words, which together with the rhyming pattern creates music.

Repetition is a device that can be used to create tension as well as music. In the first draft of a poem written in free verse, the first line of each stanza has been repeated to create this effect:

I heard a woman say
she would rather walk
and did not want to take the train,
or bus.

I heard the woman say
that 'she would rather die'
than go back with that other life
with him.

I heard the woman say

A similar effect can of course, be created by key words and phrases, as well as whole lines, while a style similar to that of syncopation in music is established by the hammering repetition of a single word.

It is a personal choice whether to keep to strict metrical patterns. Traditional poetry followed recognisable metric patterns, while contemporary poets often discard them.

One metrical system came to England from the old Germanic tribes. After the Norman conquest of 1066 there was a blending of two languages, and English poetry eventually emerged with a changed metrical system. The metrical composition of poetry is the arrangement of a given number of syllables according to certain guidelines established in a language by frequent repetition. It can be quite overwhelming when first learning these metrical tables, but it is sensible to learn the rules before discarding them. It has been said by many that poetry sings its way into the hearts of readers, and if it is remembered that metrical patterns allow the music of a poem to be remembered as well as the words, then this should assist those attempting to write poetry and maybe learning about metrical patterns for the first time.

Metre consists of a variety of accented and unaccented syllables, and these connected are called a foot. The term *foot* may have been applied because metre establishes steps throughout a poem in a measured pace.

Syllables mark the regular movements of the voice. A line

of poetry is known to scan when each line has been divided into feet, and marked with its corresponding rhythm. Four of the most commonly used metrical feet are: Iamb; Trochee; Anapaest; Dactyl. In the following explanations, lines are used to denote the applied stresses on syllables:

The iambic foot consists of an unaccented syllable followed by an accented one: as in the world alone

The trochaic foot consists of an accented syllable followed by an unaccented one: as in the word gently

The anapaestic foot consists of two unaccented syllables followed by an accented one: as in the word acquiesce

The dactylic foot is an accented syllable followed by two unaccented ones: as in the word beautiful

It can be seen that iamb and trochee consist of feet of two syllables, while anapaest and dactyl have three. There are other terms, the spondee consists of two strongly accented syllables, as in the word *childhood*, while pyrrhic has a foot of two unaccented short syllables as in *tall tree*.

If a poem is written in a very regular metre it begins to develop as a song. The less regular the metre, the more it resembles prose, although of course innovative poets have developed ways to include rhythm and a musical quality within poetry.

It is obvious that metrical patterns are helpful when a poet wishes to shape thoughts through units of measured sound. The number of feet in a line have their own names as follows:

Monometer	=	1 foot
Dimeter	=	2 feet
Trimeter	=	3 feet
Tetrameter	=	4 feet
Pentameter	=	5 feet
Hexameter	=	6 feet
Heptameter	=	7 feet
Octameter	=	8 feet

Once the names and measurements are learnt, then it becomes easier to select the music (in metrical pattern) that best suits your subject matter. A pattern can be made from whatever foot and line length you require. For instance the following line is made from four iambic feet and would be termed therefore an iambic tetrameter:

to hear/the bird/begin/the flight

A poem written in the measure of the trochaic pattern (two syllable foot established by long/short syllables, with the accent on the first syllable and an unaccented second syllable) if placed in a line of four feet would meet the definition of trochaic tetrameter.

When each line has been divided into feet, and placed with its corresponding rhythm, this is known as scanning.

It should be remembered that our speech in the English language tends to fall into the pattern of iambics. Both the dactylic and anapaestic measures can become monotonous, and this can be overcome by varying the measures.

Music can also be created in a poem by the regular beats of syllables. If lines are scanned well, often by following instinctive speech patterns, and the syllables used in a regular pattern, the regularity helps to make music and also emphasises certain points.

One of the aims of following a metrical pattern is to produce a balanced rhythm, and it can help achieve such a rhythm by reading the poem aloud. This is sometimes overlooked when composing.

All rhyming lines should contain the same number of syllables. However, since some syllables are stressed more than others (for instance the word applicable has syllables that are short-long-short-short) the result would be unacceptable to the ear. The sound made would be like a tune with no recognisable beat. It is therefore best if syllables are arranged in small groups of rhythmic feet.

It is easy when learning about metre, and what appears to be a set of mathematical tables to forget what you are actually attempting. This is of course the writing out of your feelings, dreams and experiences while trying to put them in some sort of poetic order. More than likely you will find a rhythmic quality enters your work. At times this is instinctive, but if you wish to use a rhythm in a more deliberate way then you need to work to a metrical pattern. A full understanding of the more common feet I have discussed in this chapter (the Iamb, Trochee, Anapaest and the Dactyl) will help you achieve a measured music in your lines.

To know how to scan poetry is to know how to analyse it. The best way to learn about scansion is to read a great deal of poetry, ranging through the work of such greats as Shakespeare, Keats, Wordsworth, Tennyson, Browning and many others.

To read Shakespeare is to read the best iambic pentameter. It is the most commonly used metrical pattern, and has been used by poets for centuries. Its measured pace has been found to express, in a natural way, the essential qualities that often appear in poetry: strength, beauty and dignity.

When reading your own work, check whether you have used a metrical pattern in certain lines but not in others, and make sure the pattern is regular. If you are not using a metrical pattern, check whether you have used alliterative words and whether these can form a regular sequence. Try syllable counting, you may be surprised to find that they have given you an in-built musical flow.

By exploring your own work, and that of other poets, it will become obvious that stressed and unstressed patterns of speech in a line create a concise unit to hold a thought or idea. This containment of thought can be the heartbeat of the poem. Metrical guidance in stanzas can be a persuasive factor in ensuring that readers understand and experience your original idea and emotion with the same depth of feeling that prompted you to write the poem. Free verse poetry can be just as persuasive if the poet has been in control when writing it.

Poetry does not flow out onto the page, although poetry that is well written will appear like this. The best poetry conceals the amount of work that went into the writing of it. The music within lines has been the poet's choice, and has been used to enhance the original thought that inspired the poem in the first place.

As already pointed out in this chapter, stress patterns in speech are mostly used instinctively. It is these stresses that can be marshalled into carefully controlled units, and placed in lines of poetry. These units emphasise not only the parts of language that are important to the conveying of a story, but they help to enhance images. They also help to project the feeling, and the emotive quality, that is essentially the heart of a poem.

It has been said, by those who profess not to enjoy it, that poetry is made up from words put into artificial patterns and sequences.

The techniques used by poets may well be artificial, but it is how they are used that determines whether the poem really is contrived. All the devices that have been mentioned, if used competently, can transform ordinary experience and emotion into the extraordinary.

By using technique effectively, including the technique of making music within a poem, the impact on readers can be impressive. We only have to recall certain great poems that we have memorised to be aware of this. It is often small things that are valuable in assisting the music of poetry. For instance, placing a heavily stressed syllable at the beginning of words can create a solemn mood. A variety of sounds can be created through onomatopoeia (the formation of words that imitate, or suggest what they stand for) or through alliterative clusters placed where they will make the most emphasis. None of these devices, if handled carefully and precisely, need appear contrived.

We use rhythm in our everyday speech without worrying unduly about it. The poet takes the same speech stresses, and uses them in a more deliberate way. Although this book does not set out to be a text book, I have felt it necessary to give some basic guidelines about metrical patterns and scansion. What may be regarded by some as formalities and rules can often be invaluable when writing poetry.

Difficulties present themselves if a poet becomes so immersed in the technical side of writing poetry that the sheer magic and wonder of it are lost. Never let the concern for the patterns of metre, or any other aid, take over from the inspirational moment when the poem comes in its own way and in its own time. Below is a humorous poem which is controlled extremely well. It sets out to show how muddled a poet can become when working out metrical patterns:

Disorder Discourse by S. James
Disorder is a trouble to the man
Who seeks a steady metre to his verse.

(Iambic pentameters are rather obvious. Perhaps a limerick?)

There was a young fellow from Surrey
Who had a perpetual worry;
He started a metre
Then thought it was neater
To change all the verse in a hurry.

(Altogether too flippant. Try trochaic tetrameter.)

By the windows of his flatlet
Looking on suburban gardens
Long he gazed and long he pondered
While the metres whirled around him,
Changed their form and whirled around him.

(A bit sombre. What about anapaests?)

In the heart of his poem the feeling was clear
But the beat was too definite, something was queer.

(Trips nicely, but how about Sapphics?)

Never was his mind in a peaceful day-dream,
Never could original thought be likely
While he stayed in doubt of the final outcome –
Metre or metre?

(Can't keep that up. Perhaps dactyls?)

How could he bring to the theme of his fantasy
Clothes to translate them to realms of reality?

(Oh, let's revert!)

Confusion lay upon his fervent brain:
He shunned the complex and preferred the plain.
Iambics in pentameters were fine:
Where Shakespeare led, what need of more design?

Blank verse (often confused with free verse) is unrhymed poetry in iambic pentameter. Its strength lies in its flexibility. It can change from its strict metrical regularity without affecting the rolling line. A number of poets past and present use it either regularly or at intervals. Milton, Tennyson, and Thomas Hardy have, at times, written in blank verse. The word blank refers to the absence of any rhyme at the end of lines.

Blank verse arose as an interesting innovation during the mid 16th century. Shakespeare of course shows blank verse as a tremendous medium for effortlessly conveying emotion. The regularity of such a strict pattern of music, however, can in some instances become monotonous, and it is a wise poet who at this point inserts either a slight variation in a line or creates a pause. The pause can be made by using a comma, semi-colon, or full stop in the middle of a line.

Blank verse is a strong structure, which avoids looking obvious, projects the meaning of a poem, and directs the action.

Once aware of the musical and other patterns a poet uses, it becomes easier to analyse poetry. This in turn helps the way we change and shape our own poems.

Rhythms often occur when the first ideas for a poem are being jotted down. These often come to mind because of the instinctive patterns of stresses in our speech, and can sometimes be controlled so that a well defined pattern emerges smoothly. If we rely on speech rhythms alone, where the rhythm varies very often from line to line, then the medium of free verse is being followed.

It is not easy to write poetry, let no one persuade you otherwise. Even capturing the basic idea for a poem is difficult. It takes time, and a lot of thought to write merely one poem, and if it becomes too exhausting it will prove disappointing when completed. Never let an obsession to work according to strict patterns make you deny the creative spirit. If you do so, then merely banal and poor work will be achieved. By losing sight of the instinctive process, the poem will lose something vital. This is not meant to imply that strict patterns of any description should not be used. It simply means that the arrangement of such patterns should not dominate instinct and spontaneity.

The music in the lines of a poem can induce an immediate response in a reader. Walt Whitman, the American poet, wrote in long lines which roll like peals of an organ, each line forming a musical phrase.

A contemporary poet who also seems to strike chords in his lines, has written a poem called

The Barn In Summer by I. Emberson.

The barn
contains its sorrow from the heat.
Outside
the blues, the greens, the pinks,
burn trumpets on the mind,
and the wings of swallows and hot dragon-flies
clash in a cacophony of kettledrums;
but within
there is a shimmering of muted strings,
sinking through shadows
amongst the valley-glades of wilting hay.

Short and long lines interweave to create the music within this poem, as well as the careful selection of words for imagery and alliteration. The repetition of the word *the* in the fourth line creates a breathing space between the colours being described; they have time to form in our minds before the image of *trumpets* that *burn on the mind*.

Punctuation should be used with care. In the above example the punctuation is used for effective pauses at the end of each phrase that plucks a responsive chord in us.

The words in the last three lines of this poem assist greatly in its overall musical tone. One or two, especially in the last two lines, consist of two syllables and if the poem is read aloud the musical effect is obvious.

It can be seen from the various methods discussed in this chapter, that there are many ways to produce music in poetry. Some of these follow guidelines laid down over the years. Others are new modes of expression developed as poets pushed the boundaries of their art into new areas. This is to be respected; innovation keeps art alive, and art includes the practice of writing poetry.

Poetry sets out to transform the ordinary, and the inexplicable element that effects this transformation is subtly worked into lines of words, and conveyed through the emphasis and duration of sequences of rhythm. Early man used the patterns of rhythmic dance, and primitive music, to convey themes for invoking the powers of magic. Tribal events were recorded by the use of incantations and, eventually, carols, ballads, folk and similar songs told age old stories.

As the expression of external patterns of reality, poetry encompasses all emotion and experience. It is up to individual poets to consider how to project these realities, using established and well tried methods, combined with innovative thought, as well as internal and well ordered music.

5
Traditional or Contemporary

It would be too simple to say that the poet chooses whether to write in a traditional or contemporary form. Such freedom is not always possible: the poem that seemingly comes from nowhere often dictates its own form or pattern, maybe from a rhythm arising as the words are written. The regularity of stresses in speech patterns often helps to define the measure in each line, and this in turn may help produce a metrical form.

It may sound odd to apply the word 'form' to poetry, which can be highly emotive. However, a form can be used to define an emotion or to add tension, humour, or drama to a situation.

Using a set form does not mean approaching poetry writing as if tackling an exercise, although the application of a disciplined form is one way of placing thoughts in order. It does not always follow that a poem will remain in the form first selected. It does help, however, to record the first idea for a form that presents itself because this can help in defining the meaning and emotion of the initial idea.

The sonnet, a well known form, is one way that a poet chooses to shape his thoughts. Other forms use repetitions of words, lines and phrases. These forms include the villanelle, ballad, sestina, canzone, pantoum, rondel, rondeau, roundel, and the ballade which is not to be confused with the ballad.

It helps, when writing poetry, to know something about the various forms, call them ancient and modern. Once able to recognise them, it becomes interesting, when an idea for a poem arises, to discover what form will suit it best. The form serves the poem, it helps to carry along the basic idea that is being written about.

There are varying forms you can use. The traditional ones are used either in their original patterns or adapted to suit a particular purpose. Examples of forms are given in this chapter, it is for you to decide which form serves your work best. You can of course be highly innovative and invent your own.

The ballad is basically a story within a song. In its traditional form it consists of a quatrain, the rhythm can be counted as being composed by four beats in the first and third lines, and three such beats in the second and fourth lines.

To give even more flow to the rhythm, the second and fourth beats can rhyme. Originally, ballads were composed to accompany music and dance; the popular songs of the Victorian era are spoken of as ballads. This effective musical quality can still be heard in ballads written by contemporary poets. Repetitive words and phrases combine to mark out a regular rhythm, and highlight the storyline.

The stories related in ballads, as in popular folk songs, are fairly straightforward: they range from old legends to tales of family relationships. A refrain is often quoted at the end of one or several stanzas. The repetition of the refrain obviously creates a musical effect, and this is how ballads are linked to memory.

The villanelle, written in English, uses the iambic pentameter, although this can be varied, and some poets have chosen to use the tetrameter.

It is a form consisting of five tercets with a concluding quatrain (note: tercet is the name for three line stanzas; quatrain is a four line stanza).

A simplified version of the villanelle can be created by counting syllables, but it is necessary to have the regular pattern of them throughout. I find that having guides to lines and refrains, plus the rhyming lines, helps when working to such a strict pattern.

It is important to remain aware of where the repetitive lines occur, and to help with this I use a table (rather like those used for maths) showing where the repetitive lines occur and what the rhyming pattern consists of:

First line of repetition	Line 1	(rhyme a)
	Line 2	(rhyme b)
Second line of repetition	Line 3	(rhyme a)
	Line 4	(rhyme a)
	Line 5	(rhyme b)
As first line of repetition	Line 6	(rhyme a)
	Line 7	(rhyme a)
	Line 8	(rhyme b)
As second line of repetition	Line 9	(rhyme a)
	Line 10	(rhyme a)
	Line 11	(rhyme b)
As first line of repetition	Line 12	(rhyme a)
	Line 13	(rhyme a)
	Line 14	(rhyme b)
As second line of repetition	Line 15	(rhyme a)
	Line 16	(rhyme a)
	Line 17	(rhyme b)
As first line of repetition	Line 18	(rhyme a)
As second line of repetition	Line 19	(rhyme a)

Over the years poets have tried variations on this tight pattern, for example using the repetitions essential to the form, and still retaining the three line stanza, but placing the words that end each line in the first stanza on the ends of lines of each consecutive stanza.

The original villanelle was a pastoral form which originated in France. Today it is used by modern poets as a form for a wide range of subject matter, not necessarily relating to the countryside.

Note that the repetitive lines of the strict villanelle come together to make a rhyming couplet with which the poem is concluded.

Many contemporary poets still prefer to retain the original strict form of the villanelle when writing in this pattern, as can be seen here:

Last Day by A. Chisholm

One man walks on the margin of the land
as sunset draws the blind. Another day
collapses into night beyond the strand.

Behind him, at his bidding, by his hand
the death's-head hovers. Dust returns to clay.
One man walks on the margin of the land.

He only now begins to understand
the balance of his world as it turns grey,
collapses into night. Beyond the strand

he strains to catch earth's music, whose command
propelled his soul along its ordered way.
One man walks on the margin of the land,

surveys the final tide that rakes the sand,
moon-drawn, before the moon ebbs in decay,
collapses into night beyond the strand.

One man or Everyman, he bears the brand
of slaughter where the universe is prey.
One man walks on the margin of the land;
collapses into night beyond the strand.

The poet is in control of the form here and the visionary approach is not stifled, which can happen when concentrating to a great degree on the approach to form and technique. In this instance the form outlines the meditative quality of the statement being made.

In some modern versions of the villanelle, the iambic

pentameter is sometimes changed to the tetrameter, and the refrain line is rephrased. It is a personal choice, some poets feel that the form is too artificial and that this is noticeable when set down on a page.

To an extent, all technicalities and forms used would make for artificiality, but the choice of words, imagery, and metaphors chosen helps to avoid this, and the form becomes the ship that carries the sailor home.

The sestina is a form which was originally a lyric poem, and written for singing. It has a specifically repetitive pattern, achieved by the words that end the lines. The sestina has six stanzas, each having six lines and the last word on each line corresponds to a pattern throughout the poem. It is a form either enjoyed or discarded after initial trial. It can, however, be useful in helping to contain a specific thought arising when the poem first begins. This thought may often present itself in a repeated word or words, rather than in a set rhyming pattern.

If the end-line words are thought of as colours, it will be seen from the following chart how the pattern evolves throughout the poem.

1st Stanza

Lines	Colours
1	Red
2	White
3	Black
4	Yellow
5	Pink
6	Green

2nd Stanza

Lines	Colours
1	Green
2	Red
3	Pink
4	White
5	Yellow
6	Black

The order of the repetition of the six words is on a regular system. Each succeeding stanza takes from its predecessor the end words of its lines. The sestina was originally unrhymed, but now two or even three rhymes are used if required.

There is obviously an intense pattern created by the regularity of the changing of end-line words. The poem is usually ended by a three line stanza known as an envoy, which is a small edition, rather like a postscript on a letter. In an envoy, all six word endings must recur. The traditional order for these is three on the endings of lines, and three that appear within the structure of the lines.

The canzone is more complicated than the sestina. The repetition of the same word endings is used in each stanza. This form has been used on occasions by contemporary poets purely as a discipline.

Poetical forms that use such elaborate repetitive patterns are included in this chapter because when writing poetry one word may keep hammering at the brain, emphasising the predominant image that is possibly the whole crux of the poem. Such hammering often becomes so insistent that the poet feels there is no alternative but to write the word or phrase down on every occasion that it presents itself. Knowing how to manipulate certain patterns which use repetition can help in deciding on the most suitable form.

If a poem arrives in this way, it may be found helpful to keep a note of the obsessive word or phrase even if at the beginning you seem unlikely to use it in a repetitive fashion. It may simply be a way of recording an idea that is the main concept for the poem.

When you have worked on the poem for some time, put it away. It is difficult to quote a definite time lapse, as it varies according to how individual poets work. One suggestion is to leave the poem for at least two days, possibly a week, and then come back to it with a more logical approach. Take note of a particularly obsessive word, ask yourself if it points the way for a reader to identify with the emotion or experience being related. Do some words bring sharp contrasts in sounds? If so, does this contrast intrude, or balance the poem in some way? Make sure that any devices you have used in the poem work well.

The pantoum, which is of indeterminate length, is written in quatrains in any metre with the alternate lines rhyming. The second and fourth line of each quatrain form the first and third lines respectively of the one following. Ideally, the second and fourth lines of the final stanza should be the first and third of the first stanza. However, the last stanza is sometimes changed slightly by making the second and fourth lines of the penultimate stanza not the first and third of the last stanza, but the third and first respectively. The whole poem is therefore chained together by the repetition of lines, an example of this linking idea can be seen in the following two stanzas:

Line number:	
1	*In the day as well as night*
2	*I see the beauty of the sky*
3	*I see and hear with all delight*
4	*The wonders that appear on high.*
1 (as 2 above)	*I see the beauty of the sky*
2	*In filmy clouds and sun and moon,*
3 (as 4 above)	*The wonders that appear on high*
4	*Fill my heart with nature's tune.*

If a set form seems to develop too rigid a pattern, then vary it: change words as the repetitive lines occur. You will be following the basic structure of whatever form you have selected, with your own variations included. If, of course, the stricter form suits the subject matter of your poem then adhere to the insistence of the repetitive areas.

It is often helpful to make a chart to work from when following a strict pattern. This helps a logical pattern to evolve visually as the mind struggles for suitable words and phrases. Not everyone would want to work from a chart, but with an intricate form it may help to overcome the difficulties.

Whatever happens do not lose sight of the fact that the form is your servant, and the servant of the poem. Do not let working on intricate patterns turn into an obsession.

The seeming simplicity of the triolet is delightful to use after some of the other more complicated forms. It consists of eight lines and has a short, sharp rhyming scheme. The first and second lines are repeated as lines seven and eight, and line one is also repeated as line four. Here is an example of a triolet:

The trees are tall
The grass is green,
The path is small
The trees are tall,
The leaves will fall
Before I'm seen;
The trees are tall
The grass is green.

This example was a group poem developed during a 'writing poetry for fun' evening at a writing workshop.

The rondel has a structure of fourteen lines of any length, these are usually written as two stanzas of four lines, and one of six lines. There is a refrain appearing as lines one and two, seven and eight, and thirteen and fourteen. The poem can be written in any metre, and the rhyme scheme is: abba; abab; abbaab. There is also a thirteen line structure developed by Charles d'Orleans during 1391–1466. In some cases the final refrain is confined to the a-line, the rhyme scheme of the last stanza would then be: abbaa.

The roundel, is a variant of the rondeau and has nine lines of any length. It also has a refrain which is the first half of the first line twice repeated. The poem is usually written as three verses consisting of four, three and four lines, with the refrain occurring on lines four and eleven. The poet Swinburne wrote many roundels, and it is the form he used that is most usually adopted. Here is an example:

Te Deum

I sing in praise of scented fields, and
A fire of poppies, diamond splinters of sun, the day's
Excellence, and gold light on all the land.
I sing in praise.

A child in the man, I rejoice and raise
The music of my soul, above tall poplar trees, that stand
Touching the skyline. My love I hymn through
summer's iridescent haze.

My music is love, recorded in seas and sands,
With birds winging their freedom. In a myriad ways
I sing my love, to the chant of old, old sounds.
I sing in praise.

The rondeau is a poem of thirteen lines, the first half of the first line is repeated twice, once after the eighth line, and once after the thirteenth. The rhyming pattern is: aabba; aab (and refrain); aabba (and refrain). Below is an example of this form written by one of my students, the theme of the poem is obvious:

Poetic Lamentations by G. Jennens

You bid me try a rhyme to write
On any theme I'd care to cite;
But hope evades my pencil's tip
Of any satisfact'ry quip
That would this open page delight.

What vacant thoughts could I invite
To grace this page of purest white,
And clothe the naked pencil tip,
You bid me try?

Ah! I could lead this hapless plight
Into a sense of false respite,
And in a trice then slyly slip
Beneath the notice of the quip,
This cunning rhyme of sweet delight
You bid me try!

Any metre can be used for the rondeau, and it can be seen that a regular pattern can evolve from the constant repetition of rhyming lines and the repetitive half line. This form is a traditional pattern and can be improvised upon when writing in contemporary style.

The ballad, a form written in quatrains (a stanza of four lines), is discussed fully in chapter seven.

The ballade, not to be confused with the ballad, is a poem of three stanzas of eight lines, plus a final one called an envoy which has four. The refrain is the last line of each stanza and the rhyming pattern is: ababbcbc; envoy bcbc. There are several versions of the ballade. In its early form the envoy was always used, later it was omitted and the number of stanzas increased. There is a ten line stanza form, a refrain on lines ten, twenty, thirty and thirty-five, and a rhyme scheme of: ababbccdcd; envoy ccdcd (three stanzas of ten lines and the envoy of five)

Poets writing in contemporary fashion may wish to lose what may, at times, appear to be the restraints of metrical lines. However, in some instances contemporary poetry has its own built in restraints fashioned by the counting, and regular placing of syllables throughout a poem. Alliterative devices, vowel and consonantal patterning are also often adhered to.

Line breaks or endings, are used to occur with natural pauses, or to coincide with an area of meaning. Free verse, often the description given to modern poetry, uses lines of length that the poet chooses without any formal metrical pattern. Some contemporary poetry has patterns of strong stresses that are not rigidly fixed, as well as balanced phrases. The cadences in speech patterns are noticeable as a rhythm when these are used. Slant rhymes, or echoes of rhymes are used sometimes in a pattern of slight regularity. A lyrical sense, where the poet records thoughts and feelings in a song-like way, is accepted as being traditional in idea. While a poem written in the shape that is interpreted by the poet as emphasising the theme or emotion of a poem, is considered to be contemporary in style. As for example in the following poem:

Boatrace by C. Sanderson

Desperate skill of muscle and brain
Surges her home, their airy-skimmed
Bird of a boat that slices the water
Yet seems to float, so easy the flight of her.

Here, deceptive wings of ease sustain the
Illusion that masks the effort, the strain,
The will and the heaving that stolidly pull
Through the hearts of her crew,
To their deep secret, the triumph and pain.

Note the pictorial shape of the poem, and how the vowels and consonants achieve a full flowing effect. Rather like the pulling back of arm and back muscles as the oar is lifted, as for instance in *skill of muscle*. Then on to a smooth stretch of water and rowing. The quicker effect of *surges her home, their airy-skimmed*, and in other lines *Illusion that masks the effort, The will...* And in the last line the consonants and stressed words ensure that it is read at a pace which emphasises the *triumph and pain*.

Pictorial or shape poetry may arise from the original image that occurred to the poet, and form as much of the pattern as the language.

Pictorial, or shape poems, although considered contemporary in style, were also written in earlier centuries. The 17th century poets George Herbert and Robert Herrick wrote poems that fitted pictorial shapes. Overleaf gives an example of Herbert's which is also an example of metrical expertise:

Easter Wings

Lord, who createdst man in wealth and store,
Though foolishly he lost the same,
Decaying more and more,
Till he became
Most poore:
With thee
O let me rise
As larks, harmoniously,
And sing this day thy victories:
Then shall the fall further the flight in me.

My tender age in sorrow did beginne:
And still with sicknesses and shame
Thou didst so punish sinne,
That I became
Most thinne.
With thee
Let me combine,
And feel this day thy victorie:
For, if I imp my wing on thine,
Affliction shall advance the flight in me.

If the poem is held sideways it is seen to be written in the shape of wings. The rise and fall of man, and his hoped-for resurrection in Christ, as well as the song and flight of the lark, are all depicted within a poem illustrating the wings of bird or angel. The poem has a deeply considered faith, and the mood of quiet confidence is served by the measured lines.

If the first impulse, or moment of inspired thought (which sounds very pretentious, but I can think of no other way to say this), brings with it the idea for a poem in pictorial form, then the outlines for this should be attempted as words are selected. It is not always possible to do this, in which case the picture should be sketched, with the words jotted down on a separate piece of paper; later the words can be rearranged into picture form.

Much contemporary poetry attempts to present an action, rather than simply to describe it, as for instance in single words:

He   *into the swimming pool*
   f
            e
                    ll

or

                                                        r
                                                   ve
                    mp   *o*
              u   *ed right*
The boy j   *the hedge*

In language poets relay emotions; in pictorial poetry, and what is known as concrete poetry, the idea or action is presented directly to the reader. Concrete poetry can be words inside a drawn picture as for instance looking through a window. Words for such a poem would be placed within the outlined picture of a window frame, and words placed where each pane of glass would be. In more recent years poets have experimented with concrete poetry, and presented an idea to the reader with a related picture, rather than explaining the idea through the medium of the devices normally used.

The Japanese forms have proved increasingly popular, and many poets choose to use these forms at some time. The haiku consists of three lines which contain five, seven and five syllables respectively. It does not rhyme, or have any metrical regularity. Originally, it was intended to create an image in a way that suggested a particular emotion, sometimes even a spiritual insight.

The tanka, another Japanese form, consists of five lines. The first and third lines have five syllables each while the others have seven. This form has been very popular in recent years.

Whether a poet uses traditional or contemporary forms, it is the response evoked in a reader through whatever pattern is chosen, that is important. One of the best known of traditional patterns is the sonnet. This is one of the most often used forms, it has a preciseness of metre (namely the iambic pentameter) and its length is often conducive to relaying emotion or stating something of consequence.

There are two main sonnet forms, and these are the Petrarchan, named after Petrarch who died in 1374, and the English sonnet or Shakespearean as it is commonly known, after William Shakespeare, the best known practitioner of this form.

The essential feature of the Italian sonnet is that its fourteen lines are divided into two groups with a break between them. The first group is formed of eight lines, called the octave, and the second group has six lines and is known as the sestet.

The octave usually states the theme of the poem, while the sestet in conclusion is the answer, or change of feeling. In its strictest form, the rhyming pattern of the octave is unalterable (being: abba; abba) and consists of two quatrains with the same repeated rhyme scheme. Also, in its most traditional form, the sestet consists of two tercets with repeated rhyme schemes of: cde; cde or of three pairs: cd; cd; cd (tercets are groups of three lines).

Many of the English sonnets maintain the Italian form of division into octave and sestet. Over the years a variety of octave rhyme schemes have been applied. These taken into account with the quite considerable variants in the sestet have increased the number of Italian sonnet forms. A famous Italian sonnet by John Keats is set out below:

On First Looking Into Chapman's Homer

	Rhyme Scheme
Much have I travelled in the realms of gold,	a
And many goodly states and kingdoms seen;	b
Round many western islands have I been	b
Which bards in fealty to Apollo hold.	a
Oft of one wide expanse had I been told	a
That deep-browed Homer ruled as his demesne:	b
Yet did I never breathe its pure serene	b
Till I heard Chapman speak out loud and bold:	a

– Then felt I like some watcher of the skies c
When a new planet swims into his ken; d
Or like stout Cortez, when with eagle eyes c
He stared at the Pacific – and all his men d
Looked at each other with a wild surmise – c
Silent, upon a peak in Darien. d

The English sonnet has a variable rhyme scheme, although like the Italian sonnet is written in iambic pentameters, it is divided into three quatrains (a stanza of four lines) and a couplet which concludes the poem.

The English sonnet developed from the Italian form, and a number of schemes based on seven, and not five rhymes evolved. The sonnet by Shakespeare, set out below has the rhyme scheme of: abab; cdcd; efef; gg.

If it is remembered that the structure of this and other forms is holding the entire thought process together, then those about to write in sonnet form for the first time will not be intimidated by the seemingly complicated patterns.

The final couplet in the English sonnet is often used to point a moral, or sum up. It will often be seen when reading sonnets that the concluding couplet is printed with an indentation, possibly to emphasise its function.

Traditionally there must be some relationship between the final couplet and the preceding quatrains. The sonnet form with its rhyming pattern and metrical composition, is often the way in which an argument, a statement, or a plea is presented.

Here is one of William Shakespeare's sonnets:

Shall I compare thee to a summer's day?
Thou art more lovely and more temperate:
Rough winds do shake the darling buds of May,
And summer's lease hath all too short a date:
Sometime too hot the eye of heaven shines,
And often is his gold complexion dimm'd;
And every fair from fair sometime declines,
By chance or nature's changing course untrimm'd;
But thy eternal summer shall not fade,

Nor lose possession of that fair thou owest;
Nor shall Death brag thou wander'st in his shade,
When in eternal lines to time thou grow'st:
So long as men can breathe, or eyes can see,
So long lives this, and this gives life to thee!

Note the indentation marking the couplet at the end. The rhyme scheme follows the pattern of: abab; cdcd; efef; gg.

Exercise: Try writing to this rhyme scheme in fourteen lines. Either use the strict metrical pattern, or develop it after the poem is written. Place a couplet at the final lines.

The Shakespearean and the Petrarchan sonnets are the two most popular forms. The Miltonic sonnet introduced by John Milton the English poet, has a rhyme scheme of: abba; abba; cdcdcd. Another sonnet form was introduced by the Elizabethan poet Edmund Spenser. Known as the Spenserian, this consists of the rhyme scheme: abab; bcbc; cdcd; ee.

When attempting to write sonnets, it will be found helpful to read and analyse the work of other poets. They are considered to be the most widely used forms of English poetry. The theme in the sonnet form is steadily built up, while metaphor, imagery and other devices are all used within lines. It is an intricate form, but it can be delightful to use.

All poetry can be written in either traditional or contemporary form. Poets have experimented through the ages to find distinctive and varied ways to present their ideas. Slant rhymes have developed from full rhymes, strict repetitive sequences, and rhyming patterns have been changed. The restraint of metrical lines broken.

Poets write in known and traditional patterns, or in new and inventive ways, often manipulating certain patterns to gain further freedom of expression. The pattern and form may be chosen by the poet, and both or either of these two things may direct how a poem is written.

6
Don't Wait For Inspiration

Inspiration is possibly an old fashioned word, but it is still the best explanation of how a poem arrives. However, there are always periods when inspiration or ideas do not come to mind. These are the times when a poet exists on a level concerned with matters of fact: the daily routine of earning a living, keeping house, coping on one's own, coping with a partner or a family.

If a non-inspirational period goes on for a long time a poet can experience a feeling of hopelessness. It is therefore essential to note the way we react and feel in given situations, even in the most mundane ones. It is our feelings that need to be concentrated upon, it is necessary to be aware of our emotions, for it is these that often stimulate the mind and provoke us into writing.

Inspiration is not something that can be logically worked at, it will arise in its own time. While waiting for it, there are ways to create ideas so that the essential habit of writing does not wither.

It is at times like this that reading can prove invaluable, not to evoke inspiration but to acquire further knowledge of the work of other poets. It is interesting to note the various styles and subject matter that contemporary and traditional poets have used. One subject may have been tackled by several poets in different ways, and traditional forms may have been used as sounding boards to create new methods of expression.

If it is possible, join a group of writers. It helps to become involved in discussions about poetry. Commenting on other people's work often starts up an idea for your own poetry, even if such a start seems to come in an uninspired way. Ideas can prove inspirational, and a sluggish mind can be reawakened by them.

It is customary to think that poetry has to be brought to life by living calmly in peaceful surroundings. Unfortunately we do not live in a perfect world and it is not always possible to surround oneself with beauty, or to live a life that is always quiet, ordered and tranquil.

If an eager poet is a person coping with small children, working in a noisy factory or office, or maybe driving a bus or train, it would prove very difficult to be constantly in a receptive mood for the arrival of a poem.

Yet ideas, and possibly inspirational ones, can come through even in a working environment. It may not be the same feeling that arises from a calm and meditative frame of mind, but inspiration in disguise should not be overlooked.

Years ago, I was a typist in a vast noisy office when manual typewriters were in vogue. These noisy machines were set up on wooden trestle tables placed in long rows down the middle of the room. At least two dozen typists, including myself, clattered away on these. Apart from the noise of the typewriters, and the fact that the work needed all my concentration, the telephones were also a constant source of irritation. It hardly seemed likely that such an environment would inspire anyone to write a poem.

To create a little beauty in this large bare area, someone had brought in some twigs from a forsythia. The buds were unopened, dark and mysterious. One of the typists arriving late, took off her coat, threw an incredulous glance at the dark forsythia twigs stuck in a cracked vase and asked loudly: 'Who on earth has put those dead twigs in a vase?'

The question evoked a response in all of us, and while the others explained what the apparently dead twigs were and that they would soon burst into bright yellow blossoms, my brain took stock of that moment. It became for me the essential reality. Her words, typed out were pinned on a notice board in my home. The poem that eventually came to mind was based on the connotations of the woman's question, it had evoked a response in my imagination.

Most of us have experienced occasions where small incidents suddenly appear highly significant, and when this happens it has to be recognised and used. Inspiration can come in the most unexpected ways. It was a sad thought that my typing colleague had been unaware that the beauty of the forsythia lay hidden; to her the twigs looked nothing more than drab and dead. The poem this inspired examines how a close relationship might founder if a partner was never aware of the tiny things that can deeply enrich life. Using the persona of *I* the poem was written under the title of *Nothing To Give*. Later, to achieve publication, the title was changed to *Incommunicado*:

I give you a smooth
rounded pebble,
you smile, not understanding,

I put, what you think, is a dead stick
in a vase. It is a purple-budded stem,
tightly closed against
the wintered afternoon.

I offer you a leaf. Dry,
browned, holding the past summer's sun
and watch you crumble it
like tissue in your palm.

You pull the blinds and make my tea,
turning up the radio.
I know you think I'm mad, perhaps I am?
I try to be more like you,
taking bread, spreading jam.

The news is on,
you pour my tea. It's just past six
and all the evening drapes
around us. The clock ticks.

Through the slatted blind, I see the sky
with stars hard in their brilliance.
I show you the night's velvet mesh
you shiver, pulling the cardigan
tighter round your flesh.

It's just past six, the evening darkens
round us, you have nothing to say,
and I have nothing more to give.

If only a small response is evoked by hearing a few words, the connotation they bring may spark off images. A man at a poetry workshop read out a poem he had begun in his mind whilst hammering on a strip of metal, a necessary part of his job.

A rhyme from the rhythm of his work eventually suggested itself and is set out below (although it is still unfinished):

White heat, and the beach,
and over the frill of waves white-edge
to the shore,
more and more of them

crowding one over one, and the sun over water
and beach, and bodies,
and the whispering wave on the sand, and the shouts

of children
cries of gulls mingle,
while the white heat beats, banging away in my brain,
always the same

rhythm
that slows as I tire
and the evening air cooler, the waves smoother

over the lengthening stretch of shore; and the hand
on a camera
records the day, while the children's shouts

drift farther away… away.

The inspiration for the poem came from responses to everyday sounds, the form and pace of the poem finding its expression in words and rhythms. For instance, as the man tires, the pace is made slower by lengthening patterns of vowel sounds – 'c*oo*ler, the waves sm*oo*ther' – the double syllables heightening the effect.

What if there seems to be nothing that brings the delight of a poem to mind? Try to think of this as the listening time, and use some of the exercises given in this book to keep the brain fit. Although this might not be thought of as writing poetry, it can often help to develop an idea or a theme.

A list of words or phrases for use as suggested titles can be one way of starting a poem. Get someone to write down a shortlist of titles for you, asking them to make these as imaginative as possible. Take any one of them as your first line, or make it a repetitive line in a poem. Use your chosen title in the first stanza. Concentrate on that title, why was a conscious decision made to use that particular one? Did it evoke some response, or did it bring a remembered event or emotion to mind?

Think hard about these points. From memory, a distinct picture might emerge of a place or a person. If this happens, the poem may well focus tightly on the picture. This is fine, but push the memory picture into imagery, use as much metaphor as possible. If the result appears contrived, do not be concerned; you are keeping to a discipline that may help an inspired moment to arrive.

If this non-productive time of non-writing occurs during a certain season, say the summer, try stretching the imagination, think of the opposite climate, take your thoughts and ideas into winter. Concentrate and recollect those cold, frosty mornings. Think of the first sharp, clean snow, then recall the mushiness of it. Write about the winter rain, the keen winds, and all the cold, dreary aspects of the season. Then write down the more cheerful aspects: the warmth in a room; a pub; the bright lights in shops; the good hot food; the warm bed; social events. Anyone of these may trigger off a response in your memory or imagination.

Arrange the lines, however few, that you have managed to

write on this theme into some particular form. For instance, if the whole approach is one of melancholy or gladness, a metrical pattern may help to create the mood. Note if there is a rhyme, or an echo of a rhyme, in any of the words chosen; if so try to arrange them in a regular pattern. Or count the number of syllables in the first line and use the same number in each of the next few lines. Decide whether this helps the poem along; if not, try making the regular syllable count on every other line. Note if alliteration is used instinctively, and check whether it helps the embryonic poem – if it does not, change it. Do the same exercise with contrasting seasons. For instance, springtime (full of life and vitality) with autumn (changing colours, darker evenings, natural decay).

Begin a line with the words *I remember*, and make this the first line of a poem. Go back to the photo album, or an old magazine, take note of the clothes, hairstyles, and anything else typical of a period you may be familiar with. Set out to make the poem humorous, historical or sad, and include someone you know (or yourself) in it.

The haiku form, already explained in a previous chapter, consists of three lines of five, seven and five syllables respectively. This short form can often be a way of helping a longer poem to develop. For example the atmosphere can be described in these three lines, the situation you are writing about can be set in a scene that is defined with the haiku structure. The haiku possibly begun as:

all night the wind blew
clouds scurried over the moon
tall trees stood lonely.

It could be left as a haiku because it has the correct syllable count, or it could be extended into a longer, and more descriptive poem.

For example, a student in a poetry workshop was trying to write a poem, and began with the basic three line structure after searching for ideas through an old family album:

From the photograph
My father smiled up at me
Wearing khaki shorts, drill shirt, an army badge.

The poem has moved away from the haiku structure, by losing the syllable count. It does not, as it stands, bring the interpretation of the emotion the student experienced when first looking at the photograph. It is of course, difficult to recapture a sensation initially evoked by an emotion. It would perhaps be better in this case for the poet to imagine the emotion his father was experiencing at the time the picture was taken. It is obviously a wartime picture, the khaki shorts, and army badge illustrate this. The poet could use words and lines that speak of the *smile which covers a concern at leaving home*, or a description could be applied to the bravado that can be seen in the straight back of the soldier father, and the gleaming badge. In such small ways a poem can be built up steadily, line by line. It may not be a poem directed by inspiration but, during the process of writing, it may bring back the almost forgotten phrases his father had used when speaking of his wartime experiences. The poem could be a flashback about how his father spoke of certain comrades. This, and the poet's own childhood memories about his father could become involved in the poem. A recollected glimpse in the father's eyes of sorrow, or an expression of nostalgia or joy, can also be worked into it. Memory can bring things to mind which imagination can develop into a story.

It is easy to slip into a regular pattern of simply waiting for a poem 'to arrive'. Poets often say that this time, for them, is a time of mere existence. It is indeed a waiting time, or a listening one, but if it drags on for very long, there is always the deep concern that never again will the impulse or inspired moment arrive, and the fear that never again will a poem pulse into being.

If the waiting time seems an exceptionally long one, discipline the mind. Not only that part of the mind that organises the daily rituals, and structures the language, but also its deeper recesses where its ideas are stored; the part of the mind where fantasies and daydreams flourish. This must not be allowed to become an idle part of the brain. If dreams and fantasies are elaborated upon, and moved into the pattern of a poem, as well as imaginative ideas possibly with suggestions of structures, then the whole thought process is manipulated towards poetry.

The poems we eventually write, are related to our everyday lives, in what we do, or see, or hear, and how our emotions respond to all this. It is often the way a poet meditates, on what appear to be trivial incidents, that brings an association of ideas. These may at first appear totally unrelated to the original incident or experience.

It is these small connections of ideas, often with images, that can sometimes be extended into the outline of a poem. Poets have to capture an elusive idea and encourage it to progress to another idea. The mind should sometimes be allowed to wander at will and eventually, through progressive thought, a poem will begin.

Even if this poem is unfinished, or unsatisfactory in some way, the thought process has been kept alive, and the channels for poetry will remain open.

A poem cannot be produced to order. If asked to sit down and write a poem, what you would produce on a page would doubtless be an assortment of phrases, images, rhymes and metrical patterns, plus a number of technical devices. None of this would necessarily make a poem, for although reason and intellect are involved when writing poetry, without an inspired idea, the magic will be missing.

There are times however, when ideas appear to have dried up, and impulse, inspiration, the muse, call it what you will, does not arrive. At such times certain exercises can help to stimulate the mind and increase the powers of perception. One such exercise is the use of contrasts.

As an exercise, write two stanzas of a poem, any ordinary idea will do. Compose these stanzas in direct contrast to each other, not a contrast in form or pattern, but in ideas. For example:

A love poem

1st stanza: *She did not look my way*
but turned her head, and spoke
across the room to a friend.

2nd stanza: *Later, she glanced my way,*
and fixed her gaze upon me
almost speaking out her thoughts.

Make the poem progress, using contrasting ideas and statements. One of the contrasts can then be developed further.

Exercises like this can help, but as well as practising the exercises suggested in this chapter your 'waiting time' should also include plenty of reading, mainly the work of other poets. This keeps the mind receptive to the effectiveness of poetry.

Dreams can also influence the writing of poetry. If one is lucky enough to recall them on waking they should be recorded in a notebook, and turned into poems afterwards. If the emotion experienced when dreaming can also be recorded, then so much the better. The best known reputed dream poem is perhaps *Kubla Khan* by Samuel Taylor Coleridge. The rhythm and rhyme used in this poem, gives it a feeling of spontaneity.

A poem may be created from one dream, or from several. Perhaps a place is taken from one dream, and a character from another. Some people are fortunate enough to dream in colours, these too can be recorded and used in poems.

Try to select the parts of dreams that connect in some way. This may then be interpreted as the overall theme for a poem. The emotional effect that the dream has upon the dreamer needs to be recorded in subtle ways, and not by direct statement. It is easy when recording dreams to try to rush the poem along to recapture the dream quickly, but it is the careful use of language that will bring depth to the poem, and metaphor, symbolism, imagery and other factors need painstaking attention.

Listening to music can be a considerable help when attempting to find ideas for a poem, and some poets find it also helps during the actual writing process. The type of music is obviously a matter of personal taste, although gentle music, resembling the sound of water, seems to work for many (including myself). Music can often set the theme for a repetitive line or phrase, and can even influence line length.

Different musical sounds can bring certain geographical areas to mind. For instance, if music has brought the idea of water and waves, the area can be of a familiar coastline. This can be described, taking the outlines and colours first, and building up a more general description in the body of the poem. Even if this piece of work seems to be merely a general prose description, this does not matter at this stage. The poem can be worked on more specifically later. Music is an ally in influencing ideas, and it sometimes inspires a certain rhythm that can influence the pace of a poem.

The headlines in a newspaper can be the title or first line of a poem. Notice the staccato way that journalists report events, and mimic this. Select lines that create a similar type of voice, one that has a fast pace, rapid rhythm and neat, sharp rhymes. If the headline reports violence, try to reflect this in the mood of your poem. Another exercise is to make a quick character sketch of someone, using metaphor or simile, as for example: 'A tall grandfather clock of a man' or 'The woman like a full blown peony pushed onto the bus.'

Keeping a diary is an obvious way to record events and characters, and although this will not bring magic to a poem, it can bring reminders of incidents, places and people. Interesting quotations from books and journals can be jotted down, and kept for reference, either in diaries or in a quotes file.

Through the habit of recording small incidents, as well as snippets of conversation or thought provoking lines or phrases, images are brought to mind and poems begun. Incidents, places, people and their conversations can evoke responses in us. This in turn may produce ideas for poems.

The exercises suggested in this chapter should help to sharpen your powers of observation and perception. You may not feel the same excitement that you experience when a poem just 'arrives', but there will still be real satisfaction in putting thoughts into words, and words into some sort of pattern.

The discipline of ordering thoughts and ideas, and placing them in a certain poetic form, keeps the brain supple. We have already seen how the haiku form can develop into a longer poem and there is another neat form (again Japanese) called the tanka. This consists of five lines: the first and third lines have five syllables each, while the others have seven. Here is an example:

By the river side
And in the park the old sit
All the time watching
Birds, children and animals
Deriving pleasure from this.

These lines can be extended from the form of a tanka until a longer, and possibly quite different poem, develops.

The music of a well known song or hymn can be used as the structure in which to place words, and can help create a certain mood. For instance, if the music is slow and haunting the words you choose may well be those with two or more syllables or with a vowel sequence that conjures up a poetical musical flow. If the music is jazz, or pop, the words you select will possibly be short and sharp, with lines constructed to create the effect of a steady beat. Try this, then develop your own rhythm for a poem.

A familiar item from home or place of work can be used as a symbol in a few lines of a poem. Such a symbol can set up all sorts of associated ideas: a broken doll, cricket bat, biscuit tin, tea caddy, pen, writing pad, hatstand. Any of these could bring ideas about childhood, home life, a house, the people in it. Make a list of these familiar things then write a poem in which the symbol is used discreetly, perhaps at intervals or perhaps just once in the poem.

Avoid overloading your poem with too many symbols, this way the meaning will not be in poetical form, and will be glaringly obvious.

Exercise: Enlarge upon the object you intend to write about by first describing it in prose. Write as many details about it as you want, then go over the piece of work again, and remove unnecessary detail and adjectives. Think deeply about what the object represents to you. Such thinking time is essential to poets. The representation that comes to mind is the link for your symbol. The poem will be about a particular object, the symbolism will explain to yourself, and to readers, what the object means to you.

None of what you are doing now will be wasted: memories, objects, views, can all trigger off emotions. But poetry is not just about expressing emotions, they will be there in the poetry you write, but you will transform then in various ways. Try deliberately restraining an emotive thought in a poem by using a rhythm that seems contrary to the thought. For example, if the thought is a sad one, then place your words in lines of rhythm, and rhymes as well if you wish, that make for a sing-song appeal.

Another exercise which helps the flow of ideas is to put one word on a line, perhaps a word taken from a diary or a notebook. Underneath it list a number of associated ideas, rather like this:

Bird
Call
Cat
Stalks
Settles
Flurries
Brown
Fence

The underlined words are those that have brought associated ideas to mind. The other words could equally have brought ideas, as for instance Cat, Stalks, Call. It is difficult to keep to one word only, as thoughts and images intervene. If we develop the idea of the bird and cat a little more, we may arrive at this:

Brown flurry of bird
from the tree to the bush
while the cat watches from the fence,
green eyes consider, coldly, calmly
the bird that is a brown mark...

At this stage we have just an association of ideas linking the cat and bird. Description can be added: Is it a hot day, is it raining, or windy? There must be many more definitions for the bird, other than 'the bird is a brown mark...'

Applying logical facts and descriptive words will not make this a poem, but the act of intense concentration required to imagine the given situation will heighten perceptive powers.

It is necessary to explore, to look at familiar things in new ways. Taking up some other activity at these non-productive times often helps the creative process to unwind. The activity can be centred on physical effort, gardening, athletics, or walking. Often physical effort of some kind releases undercurrents of mental activity. Playing a musical instrument, carving wood, preparing food, cooking: these things coordinate the mind and body in a similar way and release vital energy in the creative unconscious mind.

Non-productive times can be the best ones to work on those old manuscripts, even the ones discarded as not being good poems. These might now be improved, for the inspiration was there when they were first attempted. Now, with a period of quiet, logic can be applied to finding better images or devices that may enhance the poem. Perhaps the original form may be improved upon, or another used? The lines of a poem, number of stanzas, can all be thought about again. If the poem still never matures, a lot will have been learned in the process of changing it.

It does not mean that life is not pleasant if poetry is not being written. Poets, however, feel that life is a great deal happier when poetry is forthcoming. When this happens, it appears that life is more meaningful. There are times when the first impulse that brings a new poem to mind seems to have vanished. Every poet experiences the despair that this time brings. By feeding the mind with symbols and ideas through the use of mental exercises, and making oneself write when the sense of urgency is missing, the time of inspiration will come again. It may seem a long time coming, and it may also seem that the discipline and labour involved will not produce a poem.

Fly fishing, it is said, requires technique and patience. This applies also to poetry. Patience is often required during the lengthy, waiting periods. It will seem an unpromising time but, quite suddenly, a poem will come in that mysterious way that is so difficult to explain. It will flow, channelled and eventually directed by the poet, as fatigue and bleakness are forgotten.

7
Narrative Poetry

Poets are storytellers, the weavers of dreams. Telling stories involves using powers of description and observation. Characters have to appear real, and placed in situations and events where atmosphere and tension are heightened. Stories can be mysterious, fairylike, factual, or imaginary. In some way they should move the reader, some emotion in the poem should be predominant and should become the theme of the 'story'.

The dictionary definition of the word narrative is: A spoken or written account of something. If a string of words were listed, giving an account of a situation or event, this would quite logically be a narrative. But poetry demands more than this: the narrative in a poem usually has a direct style, because the story itself is all-important. However, it will be the images used, the language and form chosen that will be remembered as much as the storyline.

Stories were originally written as ballads, and the traditional ballad kept to a regular length and rhyme pattern. The stanzas were written in quatrains (four line stanzas), and sometimes included dialogue. As poetry has developed, the ballad form is not necessarily the only one now used to develop and extend a story. In fact, any pattern that the poet selects can become a structure for a narrative poem, but it must be borne in mind that, with this type of poem its chief content has to be the story.

The original storytellers wove words round some sort of rhythm, sang of heroes and exploits, and drew their stories from legends and mythology. The style is still in popular use.

Repetitive words and phrases, as well as a distinct musical quality, are the recognisable features of the ballad. After each stanza, or a series of stanzas, a refrain is used. The folk songs that are so popular are based on the ballad tradition. Poetry allows a story to be told in a concise way, with rhyme and rhythm creating music. Some narratives are unusual, mysterious and haunting, as in John Keats' *La Belle Dame Sans Merci*.

The narrative poem combines the ballad with the lyric. The former tells the story, and the latter is the musical element. Think of the poems that grip us with their storyline, they are just as rhythmically exciting. These include S.T. Coleridge's *The Rime of The Ancient Mariner*, and *Kubla Khan*, *Home Burial* by Robert Frost, *Tam O'Shanter* by Robert Burns and Walter De La Mare's *The Listeners*.

These, and many others, have gripping and fascinating stories as well as the other qualities essential to narrative poetry. By reading these, and other poems, the various types of narrative poem can be memorised, and effective use made in your own poems of the patterns you prefer and which suit your subject matter.

A strong, and evocative story is needed for narrative poems, and the music can be created by a number of methods.

Lyrical poetry is often composed in the sonnet form, as this form often expresses a deeply felt emotion. The lyric forms, which were originally written as songs accompanied by the lyre (an ancient musical instrument with strings fixed in a U-shaped frame), are not used frequently now. These forms are presented in the rondeau, ballade, and sestina.

In the traditional narrative pattern, the stories told were simple, leaving much room for the use of imagery and description. When poetry began to be printed in books, the old oral pattern of telling stories lost some of its strength. Ballads however are still a well used method of writing down a story, and many contemporary poets still occasionally use the ballad form to write out experiences.

Poets have adapted the original four and three beat lines to suit their own stories. The original pattern, was four beats in the first line of a ballad stanza, three in the second, four in the third, and three in the last line, making each stanza a quatrain rhyming on the second and fourth lines:

Once long ago a maiden fair
Fell in love with John so strong
She left her home, ran off with him
And travelled years so long.

Sometimes, when adapting the form, poets have extended the four beats to the second and fourth lines, and have made the beats rhyme also.

The basic structure and its patterns may be varied slightly by contemporary poets but they still enjoy writing within the quatrains, and often in the same rhyming patterns as can be seen in the following poem. The character written about here is included in a book titled *A Galaxy of Grandmothers*:

Crank by V. Kingsley

If she wears lace it's made by hand,
Her tweed coat is hand woven,
Her jersey's what she knits herself,
Her bread's baked in the oven.

She wouldn't touch the shop-made jam
She grows her own potatoes,
Of course she's vegetarian,
She never sprays tomatoes.

She takes cold baths, she never smokes,
She's not an alcoholic.
She is a good advertisement,
She never has the colic.

But when you hope to get a drink
It's orange juice she's pouring.
I wish she wouldn't proselytise
I like her, but she's boring.

As an exercise, try writing to any strict pattern. Take the metre as your pattern first of all, then try an intense rhyming pattern, or a repetitive style. Have an idea for a theme when you do this, and note which of the patterns and forms you use are best suited to this. Keep reading the poem aloud (one method I find particularly helpful is to dictate the words onto a tape recorder, as well as writing them down). Then listen to the poem, every stress and rhyme will jar if it is not well placed in the lines.

This exercise may determine the way you write poetry in the future. Certain forms and patterns may be found suitable for a lot of your work. On the other hand, you may decide to take a certain form merely as a guide, changing the stanza or line pattern to suit yourself. Do not be unduly concerned if you find any of the forms or patterns exceptionally difficult to master. It may be that you prefer to write your poetry in only one or two forms. Or you may even find that free style suits your subject matter better. (More about free verse in chapter eight.)

Whole lines of repetitions make refrains, and these are often used when writing narrative poetry. Too much repetition would prove monotonous, but a refrain emphasises something that has gone before in the poem. It creates a beat of music this way. Words, or particular sounds, consonants, vowels and of course, rhymes themselves, can emphasise in a gentler way what has gone before, setting up an echo throughout the poem. All of this is creating music which is important in poetry. While experimenting with this type of poetry, it may be found that the traditional narrative patterns are suitable for your poem if they are changed a little. By all means improvise if this helps your work.

The ode, a form that is included in narrative poetry, is a poem that was originally written to be sung. Ode is itself derived from a Greek word that means 'song'. It was a poem that was originally chanted, but most English odes departed from the early Greek models. The odes we associate with the poets Shelley *Ode to the West Wind* and Keats *Ode to Autumn* are two of the best known.

The epic poem is a form that is a continuous narrative. In

the traditional version it celebrated the heroic experiences and achievements of some great historical or mythological character. Two great epics, of course, are the *Iliad* and the *Odyssey* (attributed to Homer).

It is from the narrative poem that we have had legends and stories handed down to us. In this form we can take note of the imagery that is both visual and audible. The echoing sounds, through speech patterns and the devices of repetition and rhyme, emphasise this.

Here is an exercise to help establish a pattern of repetition:

Exercise: Write a stanza that picks out a word from one line, and repeats it in another, as in this example:

The moon was a silver dish
Caught in the tree's bough, its silver light
Reflecting on water where the willow shed its leaves
And the nightingale sang from the willow
and the water shone in the moonlight.

Pick out the repetitive words. Do these help the stanza at all? If not, write another stanza and move the words around, so that the repetition is used effectively. Use your own words to write other stanzas, repeating words in the structure of lines, or as a refrain.

Music and stories are two of the elements that go into making poetry, together with experiences that are part of life. Poems that carry an intense story often convey it through the music as well as words and patterns.

To get to the heart of a poem it may often be necessary to understand why it was written in a certain way. When you have tried various forms and patterns yourself you are able to understand why those patterns with awkward sounding names (like trochaic, iambic, and all the others) are used. These, and the many forms in which poetry was originally written, have been handed down to us. This is our heritage of language, culture and ritual.

When writing stories in prose it is a well known maxim

that an author should show, and not simply tell, readers what is happening. This means showing through emotions and actions. The same thing applies with poetry. Writing lines of pure description is not enough for poetry. Words have to sing their way into a reader's heart. The action in a poem's story has to be shown, and characters have to appear real.

8
Other Forms And Free Verse

Part of the pleasure to be gained from writing poetry is in the discovery of patterns and forms that suit the subject matter and their exploration. The haiku is a particularly precise and delicate form which originated in Japan. Its three lines contain five, seven and five syllables respectively and they neither rhyme nor follow any metrical pattern. Originally the lines followed the idea of what, where and when.

The haiku (discussed briefly in chapter five) has become increasingly popular with contemporary poets. It is a particularly suitable form in which to capture an impression or the impact of a fleeting moment. In its traditional pattern, it is a positive example of the use of syllables within a strict line count. Nowadays this is less strictly adhered to.

Originally the haiku always referred to a season, if not it was known as another form: the senryu. The haiku, handled sensitively, merely suggests the theme of the poem, at the same time evoking a particular emotion, or spiritual insight. It is a tercet with five syllables in its first line, seven in its second and five in its third. Here is an example:

The faded flower
brown rimmed with decay will die
exuding perfume

When writing haiku, the poet sets out to ensure that readers will see in their minds the image being recorded.

It was interesting to note, when conducting a primary school poetry workshop, that many of the children very quickly became aware that the haiku form could encapsulate a momentary emotion, or experience. For example a ten year old wrote the following haiku:

a furious wind
tormented everything near,
like an angry God.

In the structure of the haiku an image is projected instantaneously, but not flamboyantly.

Some poets now, use several stanzas in haiku form to make a longer poem:

Caught in a willow
the moon bends towards water
and hangs suspended

The lake silken smooth
holds the silvered reflection
captured cameo

The nightingale sings
before the sharp thrust of thorn
night desolation

Lost behind a cloud
the bright moon is diminished
hazy in water

Last night the moon drowned
and its broken image sank
while the world eclipsed

An improvisation on the traditional haiku pattern is sometimes used by contemporary poets, as for instance in this example by F.J. Dullaghan where an element of para-rhyming is introduced (rhyming is discussed in chapter ten):

a river flowing

golden with leaves of Autumn
Tai Chi under trees

In another poem, the same poet intentionally loses the strict syllable count, but endeavours to capture the 'haiku moment'.

stripped for the sun
potted plants trailing
shadow shawls

under the nodding
flower heads –
dead leaf curls

across the lawn
bright sun broken –
bird shadows flow

Another formal Japanese poem is the Tanka. This consists merely of five lines. The first and third lines have five syllables each, while the others have seven. The following example was a group effort by primary school children:

A Flower

Each petal is white
Lifting its head to the sun
Or droops in the rain
It is well known in the fields
Common daisy on the lawn

Qualities that help to make a poem are included in these short forms:

1) Subject and theme
2) Tone and atmosphere
3) Careful selection of words
4) Imagery

As an exercise, attempt to write a haiku in the pattern of the formal syllable count. Avoid any suggestion of rhyme. Examine the poem you have written, and note whether it includes any, or more, of the qualities listed.

Although at first these forms appear to be restrictive, it will become clear that they can be of considerable help when attempting to retain the initial impulse or original thought behind a poem. These forms require both perception and adroitness. Traditionally, the first line of a haiku set the scene, in the second line there was an introduction to something, or someone, or an explanation about this, while the last line welded the whole idea together. This form, if used traditionally, is not as easy as it first appears.

Light relief may be found in the popular limerick form. This is a short choppy poem, and has a rhyming pattern of five lines – aabba, the third and fourth lines are shorter than the others, and often precisely half size. There is no set metre. Here is an example by A. Lacey:

There was a bard from Limerick,
Who coined the word: gi – gibberick.
He wasn't a nutter
Just had a bad stutter,
This bard from Li – Li – Limerick.

Another short form is the four line rhyming poem called the clerihew which, traditionally, began with the name of a person. There are no other set rules except that the lines should be of unequal length:

Clerihew by A.G. Stump
The well known King Cole
Fell into a hole,
And said, climbing out again,
'I thought I had ended my reign!'

Not everyone chooses to write within a set form, but for those who do, and are maybe attempting this for the first time, it is suggested that they read poetry that has been written in various forms. This should help them memorise the intricate detail of the patterns involved. Examples are the rhyming patterns in the sonnet and villanelle forms, as well as the lines of repetition in the villanelle. An attempt should be made to write in a given form, but with care being taken not to become too obsessed with the technicalities of it. This may lead to losing the imaginative ideas, and other points essential to the heart of a poem. The poet Donne is reputed to have said that: 'The whole frame of the poem, is a beating out of a piece of gold.' The lustre of gold should not be dulled by the working mechanism of a poem.

If, when concentrating on a specialised form, it is found that it does not scan correctly, or a rhyme is not regular, then leave a blank space where the rhyme should occur. Try to rework the poem at a later date, checking the scansion where necessary, and changing rhyme sequences as required. Let the idea of the poem present itself, then work on the technicalities of the chosen form afterwards. Move from line to line at first, then from stanza to stanza.

Follow the chosen form, but if it seems to get lost or muddled simply keep writing down ideas, especially if images are fashioned, and suitable words and phrases come to mind. Once the requirements of a number of forms are mastered work on each of them in turn, not necessarily regularly, but simply trying to find the most suitable form for your subject matter. Try improvising on some of the traditional forms occasionally, ensuring that your own ideas, images, and emotions are conveyed.

All of this, plus reading the work of established poets, will give you a feeling for the patterns, rhymes, and repetitive sequences required when writing in traditional forms.

Examples of traditional forms and patterns are given below.

1) Couplets: These can be in any metre, but with lines rhyming in pairs.
2) Triplets: These can be in any metre, with lines rhyming in sets of three.
3) Quatrains: Can be in any metre, with lines rhyming in sets of four. The usual rhyming schemes used are

abab, abcb, aaaa, abba, aaab, aaba.

4) Quintet: A five line stanza variously rhymed, one popular way is ababb.

5) Sestet: A six line stanza. There are a number of possibilities of line and rhyme arrangement. For instance a mixture of rhymed and unrhymed lines or interlacing couplets. (Sestet is also the definition given to the last six lines of the sonnet.)

6) Septet: Very uncommon, often known as the rime royal. Resembles a ballade form. It is a flexible seven line form.

7) Octave: Eight line stanza. Could be the linking of two quatrains, or two triplets with an intervening pair of lines that rhyme aaabcccb, or a quatrain, a triplet and another final rhyme ababcccb. There can be other arrangements.

The nine line stanza is intricate in its rhyming scheme (ababbcbcc) and the ninth line called the Alexandrine is one foot longer than the rest. The ten, eleven, and twelve line stanzas are combined from smaller units and are uncommon.

Note: A particular form of the eight line stanza is known as Ottava Rima. The rhyming pattern consists of abababcc.

The Terza Rima, not commonly used now, consists of iambic pentameters which have a rhyming pattern of aba bcb cdc ded efe, and onward, ending with either a quatrain or a couplet. Written in tercets the poem flows by the linking rhyme effect.

The Chant Royal is a longer form of the ballade. It consists of five stanzas each having eleven lines, with an envoy of five. Rhyme scheme ababccddede. Envoy ddede.

The definition of blank verse is that it is a sequence of unrhymed iambic pentameters. It is the main form in the use of dramatic poetry in English, used in the plays of Shakespeare. It is a very flexible and popular form, suitable for use with almost any subject matter. It should not, as sometimes happens, be mistaken for free verse because of the unrhymed lines. It is a good exercise to practice writing in blank verse, and it helps the novice become acquainted with the iambic pentameter pattern.

Poets have experimented with these forms over the centuries, and are continually searching for new ways to express ideas and, most importantly, to communicate them. In trying to grasp with perceptive power an observation about an experience, or to relay an emotional event, or simply to make a statement, some poets have felt a need to loosen what they consider are the too restrictive patterns of traditional forms. They use what is known as free verse. By abandoning the restraint of metre, the line of poetry is no longer controlled by patterns, or stressed and unstressed syllables. Poets who use this freedom try to create the rise and fall of the natural speaking voice within their lines.

As Roger Elkin says in his excellent article on this subject in an issue of *Envoi* poetry magazine: 'Writers of free verse use cadential rhythm – the rise and fall of the normal speaking voice – to create what is called the "breathing pulse" of the poem.'

Free verse is not, as some have suggested, merely prose divided into lines. In endeavouring to find freedom in losing the strictly grammatical and syntactical, writers of free verse have a choice over the length and form of their poems. However, they do invent certain structures, sometimes in the line lengths, rhythmical patterns of vowels, the repetition of words or even whole phrases, and this helps to invoke an identification with rhyme.

If poets invent structures, can their work be defined as free? A poem will often establish certain forms itself from within as it develops. Even the idea of lineation, by establishing pauses for breathing, will develop from the sense of the words when read aloud, and create a rhythm.

Freed from the metrical line, poetry is still divided into lines, and it is the way these are placed in free verse that enables a reader to define where the poet, by the automatic reflex action of breath control, persuades the reader to pause. My poem given below as an example does not follow any metrical pattern, it is the space between lines, and the line endings, that illustrate how the poem is read:

Fox in Suburbia

He has come defiantly
through firm fences, and over shut gates
into the stillness
that lies like a drawn breath over the garden;

he waits, one paw raised
green eyes in demonic mask stare warily –
clouds trail over the moon like an eyelid closing,

trim garden corners dissolve, take asymmetrical shapes,
shocked into this new dimension
I feel his tremor, that like an unseen thought
acknowledges my presence:

he moves deliberately
yet daintily through shrubs, and young acacias,

a manoeuvre of elegance along the earth trail,
fox is a curving shadow –

dawn is his time.

When reading the poem it can be seen that the line lengths establish the pace. The occasional use of enjambment builds up the required atmosphere, and punctuation is an aid to show how the poem should be read.

Unrhymed lines of irregular length were one of the first experiments used in the writing of free verse. The imagist movement, now remembered as innovators, felt that poetry was an art that was ready to meet challenges and changes. These poets often experimented with the haiku form. They had firm intentions to lose the strict adherence to metrical structure, particularly the iambic line as well as regular sequences of rhymes.

Free verse was originally a revolt against what was considered the use of unnecessary rhetorical extras and set patterns within lines and stanzas. It attempts to avoid over-descriptive passages, and to present a whole image concisely rather than involve readers in an entire thought process. Economy was practiced in words, lines, phrasing, rhymes and devices that showed a conscious effort had been used to achieve a sense of emotion, or define an experience.

Roger Elkin endorses my own views when he comments in *Envoi*: 'In a manner similar to the handling of form, the free verse writer also abandons the restraints of metre and uses rhythm instead. Here we enter the difficulties of definition: metre and rhythm are not the same thing, nor are they necessarily interchangeable. For example, Tennyson's *The Eagle* falls predominantly into a pattern of iambs (an unstressed syllable followed by a stressed syllable). In "regular" poetry such patterns control the entire line and verse structures. Rhythm, on the other hand, is the tempo of the movement of words set into conjunction with thought and feeling. This means that the rhythm of a line or poem is dependent on the context of sense and emotion.'

His comments support my own convictions about good poetry that is written in free verse. Roger Elkin continues: 'What helps in free verse is the subtle handling of lineation, the division of the content into lines. When reading aloud or in the head, it is practice to introduce a slight pause, usually on an upbeat, at the end of a line even when the line is un-stopped: this affects the tempo or pulse of the poem.'

Much that is taken for free verse is often merely an intelligent way of using with greater flexibility, the old rules. For instance, the use of repetition other than in set lines and refrains. However, the division of the content of the lines is, in free verse, quite different from the patterned stanzas of the traditional forms. It is more difficult therefore, when using free verse, to show the reader how the poem should be read. This in turn means the meaning of the poem can be obscure, which is why the handling of lineation has to be subtly defined, as well as marked emphasis being somehow placed on pauses. These can be made to occur in the middle of lines, and at line endings. Often long indentations, or blank spaces, show where they occur.

Concrete poetry, which is discussed in chapter five, could in some instances come under the heading of free verse.

Some show an approach to regularity, not in any conventional sense but through an indication of some scansion, or sense emphasis. D.H. Lawrence and Walt Whitman used techniques, associated with free verse, that applied repetition of an expansive nature in their poems.

Walt Whitman the American poet, wrote in free verse, delighting in what must have seemed to be a new found freedom from metrical restrictive patterns. He used strident imagery, strong stresses and cadences: writing in this idiom does not mean that all devices are omitted.

There is no denying that, when read aloud, music can still be heard in a great deal of free verse. Certain words and vowels are repeated: there is alliteration, and lines containing monosyllabic words. These create rhythms that differ from those used in rhyme endings, and the strict use of units of measure. Very often the device known as anaphora is used, which is the repetition of words and phrases:

Here is a quarter moon
Here are the clouds
Here is the Northern star

Note the rhythmical, flowing movement. Try writing a few lines of poetry in free verse, use repetition in the way illustrated above, note how it alters the pace of your poem, depending on the word that is used.

When a line is too long in free verse poetry, it is tucked under the end-line, but indented to show that it is not a new line.

William Carlos Williams, another American poet, invented the three step arrangement, he wished to work in what he called the variable foot, each step equalling one foot, one pulse, no matter how many words it might contain.

Here is a student's example of this:

The white shore curves
        gleaming
                under the harsh sun

the heat glaring down
on us in our bright bathing suits
and hot skins

A poem written like this now, by contemporary poets, is often written in more lines, or sometimes less, in proportion to the idea filling them. Look at the same poem extended:

The white shore curves
gleaming under the harsh sun
shells crinkle the water line, children
squelch the wet sand by the edge of the waves.

In these lines, the student poet was hoping to establish that the effect of heat slows one down. The pace of the last line is slower to emphasise this.

It might be argued, when reading about the various methods that have been adopted, that free verse is not so free as one might have originally thought. Certainly, there may be freedom from the metrical restraints within lines, but certain structures and devices have been used in a great many poems that profess to be written in free verse.

Free verse is not merely a spontaneous outpouring, although it is often thought that the first impulse of a poem and the excitement it creates can be captured in this new found freedom. For some poets this may be true. While for others, their ideas can only find expression in more traditional patterns. Poets must decide these important issues for themselves.

Poems written in free verse have their own qualities of strength, which can often be seen in the lineation of stanzas. For instance, some free verse poetry is written in short lines. This way the attention is drawn to the deliberate omission of metrical patterning. Short lines can also emphasise the statement-like quality of some poems. Enjambment, a device already spoken of in this chapter, is also well used in free verse. The use of this device enables a line to spill over to the next without the use of punctuation, as in the following example:

We are the lost ones, here on this
Vast planet, we are
the lonely ones
waiting...

Enjambment can also help to create tension, by building up the emotional effect at a fast pace.

Free verse is not simply 'throw it on the page line by line' sort of poetry. It endeavours to capture a sensitive response to content, shaping lines according to both the meaning, and the emotion.

Many poets experimented with free verse, and poets who were the innovators of this wrote on all subjects. These include the intensely personal, the bardic and the emotive.

Although poets may consider they have removed certain restrains that inhibited their work, it will be seen when reading some free verse that it is not necessarily formless. The main consideration of those who first wrote in this way was to remove the iambic line.

Try writing without the use of formal patterns. Do not use regular stanza patterns, replace these by lines that are irregular in length and pattern. Develop the idea you may have for a poem in this way. Use alliterative words rather than strong rhymes on line-endings. If you experience difficulty in writing this way, begin with the three line haiku and develop your thought from this. Try using monosyllabic words in some lines, or the three step arrangement already discussed in this chapter. Use repetitive phrases which can bring the similarity of rhyme to a poem. Use punctuation within lines, and not necessarily on the end of them. Shape your poems, make them thin, or wide whichever way relates best to the subject matter.

Music often develops in free verse poetry by the use of vowel sounds that are patterned skilfully, as in the following example:

Gift by M. Pain
I will walk
lightly
over small stones.

The great nights
and thin rain
do not deter me.

You have lent me
a broken time,
my love turns
on a point of
silence.

I will leave
a black remembrance
at your door.

It will be seen, and heard if the poem is read aloud, that thin vowel sounds have been used in the first two lines, as in the words *will* and *lightly*. These thin vowels are used elsewhere in the poem with full effect. The lines are short in length, which creates a visual preciseness. There is a contrast in sounds created through the placing of words that contain resonant vowel vibrations. The softness of certain letters, as for instance *m* in the third stanza, and the sibilance of the word *silence* convey the sense of quietness the poet wished to achieve.

Note the word at the end of the third stanza that is tucked in to show it is not another and separate line. This makes a delicate yet definite effect. The vowel sounds in this poem link with the inner sense of it.

In the next poem enjambment has been used, and again vowel patterning is employed to good effect. Consonants create the effect of the flow of the sea, and a smooth rhythm is contained throughout the poem. Note how the letter *s* helps to achieve this:

Ebb Tide by P. Poole

The tide ebbs slowly
leaving isolated pools
open to sun and wind
where minute sea-creatures
at once sense peril.

Cockle and tellin shells
swirl and swirl again
grind deeper and deeper
into sand. As a child
snuggles beneath bedclothes
they seek sanctuary, hidden
from beaks and crunching feet
safe until the tide returns
and the certain sea
washes them to new danger.

There are many forms in which poets can choose to write, and a variety of free verse definitions that can be elaborated upon. It is for the poet to select the form which will best suit the poem being written.

9
Poetry As A Way Of Life

To be totally committed as a poet is rather like being a perpetual apprentice; perpetual, because the apprenticeship never ends. You can acquire skills in the use of forms, techniques and language, but this is to become a maker of poems and not a poet. Poems are inspired from events and experiences combined with imagination. It is by these ingredients in relation to one's own psyche that the poet is motivated to write.

Poetry produces a kind of magic, and today's society understands that the poet's thought process, once considered illogical, is of value. The perceptive powers of poets work in ways that, to many, may appear odd – but they still work.

Poets have a type of reasoning, as well as a language and thought process, that appears strange to many people. Poets, however, know (or learn) that it is this very type of reasoning that enables them to reach into depths beyond the sense of every day logic.

Intuitive thought plays a vital part in the power of art. Moments of intuitive perception are, to poets, the moments of reality that convince them that their thoughts are as logical and rational as those of the scientists.

What does all this mean to those who write poetry, but have to earn their living in other ways? Even if your poetry is published, it brings no great financial reward. So it is not practical to sit at a desk waiting for the muse to visit, most of us have to earn our living in other ways.

Whatever ways poets earn their livings, and no matter what their circumstances or backgrounds, they will always find a way to write, for no other reason than that they have to. Ask any poet about this. The answer will invariably be that they are compelled to write. Without writing, poets are left feeling desperately unhappy.

On the other hand, as every poet is aware, the times when a poem is 'on the way' is a time of exultation.

To earn a living, poets may have to work in an environment to which they feel totally unsuited. They may cope competently enough but their particular talents, which are useful when writing, may not be drawn upon during a working day.

It is difficult in such situations to avoid the feeling of frustration that a working routine brings, when one would rather be sitting in front of a typewriter or word-processor composing poems. However, the perceptive powers are always at work, and a note can be made of small incidents that might go into poems. These can be retained in the memory, and recorded when free from the working day routine.

This is where the poetry workshop, or readaround, can be beneficial. If in your area there is somewhere poets meet to relax and discuss aspects of poetry, then do go along. Those incidents retained in your memory can, with help, be moulded into the forms and shapes of poems, and in this way poets can remain convinced that all that they write has some worth.

It is not simply how much poetry someone has had published that makes them a poet. It is the total commitment to the waiting period, or the conscious effort to apply poetry even in the most ghastly of situations. For instance, Irina Ratushinskaya, and others who have been interred in labour camps, produced poetry in the most terrible circumstances.

Those who are aware, or who are possibly beginning to accept, that poetry is a way of life, may have discovered that it is the continual assessment of many things relating to one's own psyche that encourages creative energy. Those who doodle or who, as they tell me, 'lick a poem into shape' on a bus or train journey are not poets. They may enjoy the challenge of manipulating language, but do not have the same process of thought as those who are committed to poetry as a way of life.

Certain jobs may seem to suit the talents of poets. Something in publishing perhaps? Or in any field of art, or teaching? Inheriting a large legacy might prove even better. Everywhere the grass is greener, yet every situation or job probably entails the acceptance of responsibilities that exhaust the creative urge. It is not, of course, advisable to give up regular employment and take time out for the muse to visit. There are poets, and other artists, who have made a decision to work in the capacity that best suits their inner needs of creativity. One poet of my acquaintance is a gardener, another an odd job man, and a third is a door to door salesman. These jobs enable them to work at hours to suit themselves.

Poets are numbered amongst teachers, insurance agents, miners, shop assistants, office and factory workers. There are also bank officials, drivers, nurses, farmers and social workers who are poets. The list is endless. When it is necessary to work to earn a living, then it is also necessary for poets to learn how to compartmentalise their minds.

This might appear to be recommending that poets take on dual personalities, and so it is in a way. We all, to some extent, wear a mask and keep our real feelings hidden. These feelings can be released when sitting down to write poetry. To be totally and intensely focused on the moment of perception is what every poet desires. To be able to recapture and illuminate that moment it is necessary to become another person, away from the regularity of whatever employment takes so many hours from the writing time each day.

The recapturing can often be achieved through certain routines. If it is possible outside working hours, try to find ways for relaxing the mind. Meditation is one way. Simply try to focus the mind on an object or a certain view, and let all the problems you may have encountered during your working day be erased from your mind. Taking a walk often helps, it does not need to be a long one. A swim, either in the local baths or in the sea if you live near it, can relax the mind. A short while spent in the garden, either working or sitting there, can help. Listening to a favourite piece of music (use a personal stereo if your choice does not blend in with the rest of the family's).

Just being silent can be rewarding, it is a way to quieten the brain from the activities of the day. During this time images of people and places may come to mind that may eventually be used in poems. Try not to get too relaxed, this period is merely to bring to the surface that part of the mind known as the creative unconscious.

It is best if a habit of relaxation is used regularly. Afterwards, you will find you are able to write about not only a certain incident that you noted during the day, but you are able to record your emotional response to it. This does not necessarily mean that this incident, or a special moment of perception will be recorded in a poem on the same day it happened. It may not even become part of a poem in the same week or month it happened. The best poems take time to develop.

The waiting period, when moments of perception, or a state of heightened awareness do not seem to exist, is the time when poets can experience depression. Poets have a need to record sensations in language. Literal interpretations are placed by them on images during creative periods. Without a heightened sense of perception which produces ideas and images it is easy to feel that the world is a void.

Inspiration, spoken of in a previous chapter, is inexplicable. It is the longing for it and the waiting period that has been known to drive poets towards madness, or to excessive drinking, or possibly to make foolish and irrational choices and decisions. It is of no consequence that a poet has any other occupation at this time, for the waiting seems a lonely and unfulfilling period. No matter what is achieved in other areas, this arid time seems to be hopeless. Worse than this, it appears to be endless. It is a time that poets understand all too well.

During such a time, the exercises that have been discussed elsewhere in this book, and the suggested ideas in this chapter on how to relax the mind, can help. What is happening when these things are practiced is that thoughts are being turned inwards, into the private world of recollection, reflection, memory, fantasy and imagination. Do not be impatient for a poem to arise, for the best poems come at their own time.

It is necessary for the apprentice poet to understand that poetry demands so much. It is, however, bewildering to discover at the start of the apprenticeship that there will be periods when a sensation of loss and depression occurs. Be patient during these times that seem devoid of any ideas for poems, and enjoy all the more the occasions when a poem arrives.

When a poem is nearby, and arriving after a long period of total blankness, it does make itself heard, but the poet has to be listening. The following is a poem of mine about this very subject:

A Shadow

The poem said 'listen',
I thought I heard the sound of water
running over pebbles, like a muttered
echo of some truth escaping.

I listened, waiting,
and seemed to hear the invocation
of some rhythm, as in a shell's
tight curl.

And waiting, silent,
felt the nearness of a shadow,
and heard a heartbeat span a space
between the earth and heaven.

A poem is an exploration of oneself, and one's intuitive faculties. If a poem does not come for a long while, and a poet is not called upon to use these faculties, then a sense of loss is experienced.

At these times of waiting, other creative activities can be enjoyed. Take the mind into areas that have nothing to do with writing. Some poets paint, or carve wood, or garden.

Playing a musical instrument often releases creative energy, as does the enjoyment of cooking or embroidery. Sporting activities, reading, listening to music are all good diversions at such times.

It is easy at this stage of creative non-production to find, after reading the work of other poets, that you imitate their style. To take the opening line of a poem, and to develop one's own idea from it, can be an effective exercise to stimulate sluggish thought. Be careful, however, not to copy lines of the poem completely in your own rough drafts. The exercise must be used simply as an attempt to produce an imaginative idea of your own. Whatever you write must not be a replica of any work by another poet.

Why does it concern poets so much when they are unable to write? It is because, as a way of life, poetry involves every part of a poet's senses and intellect. If a poet loses the time of inspiration, and does not have the excitement of new poems arriving, then the emotive response to events and people appears lost.

This happens at some time to every poet. During this time, when visionary and inspirational sensations are lacking, it is possible to lose the conviction that you are able to write poetry. To survive during this period, do use the exercises given in this book, or any others that you have found helpful, and induce the right frame of mind for productive and creative output.

The channels of poetry can be kept open by helping others to write it at poetry workshops. It is difficult, even impossible, to understand why the writing of poems matter so much. It is certainly difficult to explain this to those not interested in writing poetry. Life for a poet certainly assumes a much better outlook when inspiration is plentiful. Poetry dominates, for it is the master, and the poet the slave to its demands. This, of course, is felt most strongly when writing in the heat of an inspired moment.

There is no logical explanation for why poetry becomes a way of life. Poets simply write because they have to. They deal in equations of happiness, grief, and the general experiences of life. These truths are expressed in poetry through ideas, images and language, which throughout the centuries have expressed the values of human life and experience.

Helping others to write poetry is a good idea. It keeps your mind receptive to poetic thoughts, even if for a time they are the thoughts of others. By discussing and reading poetry, the creative unconscious mind is stimulated.

This chapter is not intended to imply that poets are not normal or average people. It is necessary though to understand that a chance word, or some small experience, will assume great significance for a poet and become something that needs to be written down and conveyed through the poetic mediums.

Poets number amongst artists who have, over the years, been imprisoned because they expressed truths and values that had become neglected. A number of poets have been imprisoned for speaking honestly; Irina Ratushinskaya was sentenced to serve twelve years for the crime of writing poetry. She was sent to hard labour camps and endured great suffering. Finally, released from prison in Kiev in 1986, she was allowed to come to Britain for medical treatment.

These poets are tackling the big themes, but most of us write about the small incidents or experiences. We write about things that, when they occurred, appeared to be major realities in our lives. The impulse of those times, or the inspiration in those moments brings the concept of a thought, and to the poet this will appear in the outline of a poem. Blake, Milton, Shelley, Yeats, and many others, had inspired moments. Does this imply that poets are visionaries, and in some cases prophets? In the moment of inspiration, they become so.

Poetry is not achieved merely through a conscious arrangement of words, it comes from the inner depths of emotion and understanding. Poets need to be sensitive to their own surroundings, and to people. They have, it is said, a third eye, but a skin less.

The daily routine of looking after a home, earning a living, or doing whatever fills the working hours, can dull perception. If this is found to be happening, it is then vital to find ways, however small, to make sure that perceptions surface.

This can be seen and heard in the way children comment on something that may seem so familiar to us that we hardly notice it.

For example, a young schoolboy told me about his trip to the seaside. It had been high tide, and the waves were quite large ones, the sea could only be described as choppy. Each incoming wave, he told me 'had been fastful'. Not sure of what he meant he was asked to spell the word 'fastful'. He wrote it the way it is printed here, and explained. 'We say something is beautiful, but those waves were fastful'. Splitting the word we discovered his meaning: literally – fast, and full.

He was presenting an image and, during a workshop session, was persuaded to place this image in a line of poetry. He found that the word made more impact when written as *fast-full* and was surprised to be told he had coined a word, something he had not been aware he could do.

Children notice things in an enthusiastic way. Try to look at objects as they do. For instance, take note when out shopping of the bright colours of fruit and vegetables, packets and tins. Write these colours down in lists when you arrive home and try working some of them into one or two stanzas, trying to use metaphor or simile when describing them.

Observe the people with whom you work in more detail. Note the way they walk, or the way they move their hands. Do they look pensive, angry or placid? Note how the expressions on people's faces change when they talk. All these observations may well make their way into poems in the future. If you can, try to note down such observations either in prose or in the form of a poem. Try comparing a person with an object (an idea already suggested as an exercise in another chapter) because comparisons often point the way to more detailed descriptions.

Try to make your notes at a regular time, this will help the brain to recognise that it is a writing time. Such an ordered way of writing may seem a chore and unrelated to writing poetry. It will however, eventually prove to be a considerable help in avoiding the dreaded writers block.

These exercise periods may not produce poetry as we

think it should be written but they certainly provide gymnastics for the perceptive and creative unconscious mind. The mind can become tired, lazy, or just indifferent to the events of an ordinary day. Without the impact of the moment of inspiration, it is difficult to maintain the outlook necessary for poetic creativity.

It has been said to me during a poetry workshop that it is best to wait for a poem to arrive, and that the enjoyment of writing poetry can be lost by the use of such exercises and regular routines. The exercises discussed in this chapter are intended for use during the time when a poem does not arrive. They can also prove helpful where a daily routine does not otherwise include any aspect of writing poetry. It is important to remain alert and receptive to incidents, events, or whatever else needs to be recorded for later use in poetry – and to do this the mind does occasionally need to be disciplined.

Familiarity in the way one sets out to write anything, whether it is the title, first words, or first line of a poem, can be established by a certain routine. This can condition the mind to realise the creative process is about to begin and is an invaluable discipline. Your routine can evolve from such perfectly simple acts as sitting at the same desk at the same time every day, or by writing a few words at the same time each day – perhaps early in the morning, at lunchtime, or last thing at night. Do not write at length at these times, just a few words or lines to keep the creative flow moving. Whatever method you use when composing, either handwriting, typing or using a word-processor, stick to the same one and let the brain become accustomed to the routines of your method.

The organisation of thoughts and words at such times persuades the mind that you mean business. The routine, once it becomes familiar, is a discipline that helps you to think about writing even if the actual appearance of a poem has not occurred. It will appear eventually because the routine and familiar pattern will help the creative unconscious mind to respond to other stimuli.

These stimuli will be provided by the notes you have

recorded about events and characters, and your involvement or responses to these. The following idea is presented as an example: You may have seen a look of anger on someone's face. It may have been at work, or at home. Try to imagine why this look surprised you so much. This small incident can set up a wealth of connotations, and the idea can be extended in various ways: Let us, for example, imagine that the look of anger surprised you because this particular person is usually very placid.

Try to imagine how you would feel; surprised certainly, and possibly shocked. Why was this, did the look jolt a certain memory? Some person from the past who also surprised and shocked you by displaying anger? This is a hypothetical situation, and one based on imagination, but similar events happen everyday, be on the look out for them.

Poems can surface from incidents and memories. It is through the recording of such incidents, however trivial they may seem, that activates the imagination. However tired, and however sluggish the creative mind has become, once perception is sharpened by certain stimuli the creative process will begin.

Revision, and re-shaping a poem, can be done in a time outside the set routine. Finding the correct rhyme, pattern or form and continually sorting and sifting to find the exact words required, is a different part of that initial concept.

This chapter is about poetry as a way of life, and how to keep the mind stimulated during periods when a poem does not arrive. Some of the methods given as examples should prove helpful in preventing the powers of perception from becoming dull.

A true poem may take a long time before it presents itself, and a poet may have concerns and problems in life that prevent any creative thought developing. A job may be lost, a marriage problem unresolved, a hospital visit undertaken, or a report written. All of this takes time the poet would rather use writing poetry, for poetry is the sustaining factor in a poet's life.

At the times of waiting, when it seems that a poem is never likely to be written again, it may bring some comfort to reflect that the creative unconscious mind might be taking a rest. Mental powers, just as physical ones, get strained and need to recuperate.

A poem will surface eventually, it might be brilliant, it might not, it will certainly have been worth waiting for. Everyday experiences can be used in poems in whichever way a poet chooses. The poet can place these, as well as events and people both real and imaginary, in poems in a strident or delicate way. The language chosen can increase the pace of the poem, or make its tone gentle.

Everyone who writes poetry will know of that strange moment of utter stillness when a poem is brought to life. It is the time when the mind seems frozen in a moment of perception.

The poet presents an added dimension to life through words that imply a closer contact than the physical with experiences and events. The poem is worth the waiting, and it is this waiting which is part of the poet's way of life.

10
Rhyming Patterns and Rhythms

One important thing to remember is that poetry does not have to rhyme. It is often mistakenly thought that, unless it rhymes and chimes, it is not poetry. Rhyme, when used, occurs because two sounds that are similar are placed so as to create an echo with one another. It is not necessary for rhymes to be always placed at the end of lines. They can be placed within lines also, and this will be discussed as the chapter develops.

The rhymes that are known as full rhymes include the following:

Masculine Rhymes: These are one syllable rhymes occurring on the stressed syllable, for example: *bard... lard* and *lent... sent*.
Feminine Rhymes: These are two syllable rhymes which are heard to good effect when a line of poetry ends on an unstressed syllable, for example: *lapping... trapping*.
Rime Riche: These are created by the repetition of a word which has more than one meaning; the first time the rhyming word occurs it carries one meaning, and the second it carries another. Examples are words such as blue (as in colour) and blue (as in emotion, depression), or kind (gentle and considerate) and kind (as in a class of similar things, for example mankind).
Three Syllable Rhymes: These occur in such examples as *precluding... excluding*. Obviously, the more syllables that are used the more variations in rhyme are possible.

At times, poets have been known to use masculine and feminine rhymes in alternating lines to create a distinct melodious pattern:

In the island of living
And joy of being free,
There is taking, and giving
Always 'twixt you and me.

The ballads (discussed in another chapter) had a regular, well known yet simple pattern of rhyme.

If the following example is read aloud it can be heard how a musical jingle is created by the rhyme:

I'll take the road to my love
As one in love would do
I will walk the whole way to her
And my love will know I'm true.

Nursery rhymes, poems that relate stories or pass on information, are mostly created in effective rhyming patterns. These are effective because they help the memory to retain information. One rhyming sequence learned at school creates music as well as defining how the days of the months can be remembered:

Thirty days hath September,
April, June and November,
All the rest have thirty-one
Save February alone
Which has twenty-eight days clear,
And Leap Year coming once in four
Gives February one day more.

The use of alliteration can also create music. Alliteration is the repetition of the same consonant sound, a device very commonly used in Old English and Medieval poetry. Alliteration is still used a great deal today, probably because it is built into the natural speech patterns of the English language. It often slips quite easily, and sometimes instinctively, into lines and phrases.

An example of alliteration would be: Clean cats can cry. Consonants are also used for repetitive rhyme effect in places other than at the beginning of words as for example in: When cats dictate by cries the time they can be fed.

This subtle way of using alliteration is sometimes more suitable for poetry than the direct and more obvious sounds of exact alliteration, used at the beginning of words.

Poetry is made effective in its music by the distribution of sound patterns. Not only do these achieve music, they are also devices which enhance tension, atmosphere and emotion.

Alliteration can be used subtly, and this way it will not create echoes and rhymes within a poem in a blatant manner. Used selectively within line structures, it will create effects in a more natural way than the development of some line-ending rhymes. Although these too, if used carefully, can be as useful a device as alliteration.

The poets who often wrote, and those that still write, in the medium of blank verse have their own reasons for doing so. Blank verse is poetry that is unrhymed but follows the regularity of the iambic pentameter although originally it meant unrhymed poetry of any metrical length.

Rhymes, like those used in nursery rhymes and ballads, can often be limiting in their effect. They do, of course, create excellent melodies and are useful aids to memory. Apart from music within a poem, rhyme creates a response in a reader's mind: the initial rhyme sets up a strong expectation in the reader's ear of an echoing pattern to follow. To avoid what some poets think of as a rather limiting effect, rhymes can be placed internally in a poem – within the lines, as opposed to being placed on line-endings. This method of rhyming, if used correctly, can set up echoes and create rhythms, as in this example:

Letter to Aunt Jane

Today, I will write to Aunt Jane,
she is old and alone, my letters form part
of her pattern of living.
I shall mention the rain,
cost of a new winter coat – and the relatives.

I cannot speak of famine in Africa,
or refugees along borders.

It's not easy writing to Aunt Jane,
for in 1916, when her brother was killed
somewhere in France, she became aware of a sorrow
shrouding a nation, pinned up her hair
and lost the joy of her childhood.

She drew apart from us, fading gently
until another war involved her, and hearing
of the death in a plane of her younger brother,
she grew suddenly old.

The British Legion and prayers in November,
brought her no understanding. She remained solitary
restricting her life to the habits of home,
a walk down familiar streets, and her library book
once a week.

Why should I speak of the bomb, the threat of
uncertainties? I shall talk only of holidays,
of making jam, of children growing older.

I shall span the pages with inconsequential things
I will not destroy the myth of her realities.

By analysing this poem, it is obvious when the word'Jane' in the first line is said aloud, that it is accented, and the reader would almost instinctively respond to the consequent echo in the word 'rain' in the fourth line of the first stanza. This sets the pattern that flows on into another stanza, for instance in the fourth stanza, the third line and the word 'plane'.

The poem does not employ a regular pattern of rhyme, but it does have this echo which is used for rhythmic harmony. The break from this echo in the fifth stanza, was quite deliberate, as the harshness of the overall theme of the poem is being emphasised in this way. The disruptive pattern changes the harmony abruptly, and signals an alteration in the tone of the poem the echo occurs again in the last two stanzas.

Having discussed alliteration, which adds rhythm as well as partial rhyme to a poem, now is the time to refer to another device which is commonly used for similar effect.

This device, known as assonance, is where the repetition of vowel sounds is used to make half or near rhymes. These rhymes can also be used with full rhymes, and some contemporary poets do use this combination.

Assonance differs from alliteration because it occurs through the similarity of vowel sounds in syllables that do not form a complete rhyme. As for example the long *o* in *home* or the short *u* in *sun*. This device, if used, requires careful thought, for vowel sounds are often marked by the effect of consonants that are adjacent. However, it can be as forceful as a full rhyme when the vowel sounds are placed on line-endings.

First world war poet Wilfred Owen needed new ways to express his intense feelings of anger and compassion about the slaughter of young men in the front line trenches. He used assonance and manipulated it powerfully, together with other devices, to achieve an emotive response not only to his tremendous technical abilities but also to the horrors of war.

Wilfred Owen is considered to be the innovator of partial rhyme, known as para rhyme. An example occurs in the last few lines of a stanza from his poem *Strange Meeting*:

Lifting distressful hands as if to bless.
And by his smile, I knew that sullen hall,
By his dead smile I knew we stood in Hell.

In para rhyme the consonant sounds of the two echoing words are the same, but the vowel sounds differ, (as in the words *hall* and *Hell* in the lines above). There is a slightly discordant sound about para rhyming that suited the painful subject matter of Wilfred Owen's war poems.

These para rhymes, when used competently, weave strict patterns that are as formal as the traditional and commonly accepted full rhymes.

Partial rhymes are often used in contemporary poetry

because they seem to serve its purpose better than the more strident clamour of full rhymes. Examples can be found in words that have unstressed rhyme and end in consonants that are also unstressed.

Trailing rhyme is used when an unstressed syllable trails after its rhyming one as in the following lines of contemporary poetry:

The man reached up and made the street light
flare, the gas lamp roared,
and children ran indoors to brighter
rooms.

Rhymes form interesting patterns, and there are many forms apart from the well known ones that appear on line endings.

In one of my poems given as an example below, musical sounds are distributed by the vowel and consonants patterns throughout the stanzas:

Arbor Low (Stone Circle, Derbyshire)

Some other dream
silhouetted under Moon
and Northern star,
laid its haunting time
upon the sleeping stones,
undeciphered runes of whispers
drawn through silences.

Some other dream
distanced from our time,
caught the incense of moorland air
the pulse of summer,
fall of water from a distant crag –
as green on gold, the tigering day
streaked the white markers
of antiquity.

Some other dream
enacted out our own,

breathing an incantation that threaded
rhythms of three thousand years,
between the circled stones.

Some other dream
woven in echoes,
like a litany
of souls,
hallows the timeless mystery
of the centre stone,
and waits through silences.

The word *dream* in the first line is an extension of sound created by the two vowels *e* and *a*, this is echoed by the two *o* sounds in the word *Moon*.

The sound pattern is further extended by the use of the double *e* sound of the word *sleeping*, while 'undeciphered runes of whispers' makes alliterative use of the letter *s*, and the soft *c*. This alliteration is further enhanced by the last word of this stanza *silences*.

Again the soft *c* in this word, together with the previous soft *c* acts as reinforcement for the sounds of *s*, all of which creates a slow dream-like pace.

The word *dream* sets the same pace in the second stanza, but this time the hard consonants break the dreamy pace and it becomes noticeably quicker, particularly in the latter part of the stanza.

The softer consonants in the third stanza bring back a little of the early dreamy pace, although here the alternating hard sounding consonants keep the pace varied, preventing the dreamy effect from becoming monotonous.

The last stanza of the poem again combines the soft and hard sounds, that is until the final three lines when the poem, through alliterative rhythm, assumes a tone of reverence.

It can be seen when reading the poem that the alliterative pattern creates the rhythm throughout, and that the rhythm is reinforced by the assonance. In some instances unstressed rhyme is used, as for instance in the echoing words *day* and *antiquity*. An echoing rhyme is achieved in the final stanza by the words *litany* and *mystery*.

It obviously helps the would be-poet to read and analyse poetry. It is also a considerable help in the writing of one's own poems to understand why certain rhymes achieve better results at times than others. Rhymes should never be made too obvious, this will detract from the general theme of a poem, particularly if it is a serious one. It would be very difficult for a poet to change certain lines that were slipping into pure doggerel if unaware of how such devices as rhyme, alliteration and assonance are deliberately used to create effects.

There is a tendency to be too slack when using rhyme, and this is something to check when revising a poem. It is easy to be so caught up in writing out the meaning and form of a poem, that the selection of the best rhyme is not carefully thought out. The first one that comes to mind may be used without realising it is not the best choice.

For example the word *love* needs more than the word *glove* to enhance it, and *June* and *moon* and *night* and *bright* are two more examples of obvious rhymes.

Clusters of words, like *poses of roses*, that so obviously rhyme will not stretch the mental capacity of either poet or reader. Rhymes require very careful thought, and must then be structured well within a poem or on the line endings.

A traditional pattern of rhyming, still in use today, is the rhyming couplet. This consists of a two liner, often a section of a poem, which can have a complete meaning within itself. The terza rima consists of a series of tercets, which is to say written in three lines. Each stanza of a poem in this way is linked to the following one by rhyme. The poem written in this style usually ends with one separate line or couplet. The terza rima sonnet has four tercets and ends with a couplet.

Sprung rhythm, which was initially used by the poet Gerard Manley Hopkins, has features that resemble free verse as well as metrical. It is similar to the pattern of metrical poetry because it has lines that have a number of recurring stresses, but as in free verse it uses rhythms of speech. This daring innovation has greatly influenced contemporary poetry. When reading the work of this poet it will be seen that certain rhymes are made by borrowing a sound from the following line.

Rhythms can similarly be effectively created by the arrangement of stanza patterns, and this is too often overlooked when writing poetry. For instance, if a stanza is regarded as being somewhat like a paragraph in that it establishes or develops an idea, then the end of a stanza can create a pause. The pace of a poem can be deliberately changed from stanza to stanza, either by using words with long syllables alternately with short syllabled words, or by changing from long to short clipped words. The sound pattern will be effectively heard to change when the poem is read aloud.

A rhyme will often lead the reader into a poem, it can persuade a reader's senses to follow the internal meaning. Rhythm is also a persuasive factor. Repetition is another extremely effective medium for creating rhythm, just as alliteration and assonance are. All these devices can be seen to work in this poem:

The Ringing of Pigs by L. Richardson

One cannot forget to feed pigs.
They squeal like children on the rack.

But the ringing of pigs,
The catching and holding of their leather ears,
The cornering and holding of their handle tails,
The being held upright between knees,
The indignity of ringing;
That is another matter.

Under the long white lashes,
The backward glance
Of the watery blue eye
Beseeches clemency.

The pencil-sharpener nose
Blows out droplets of fear.
But the metal's sharpness dents the gristle snout.
The pincers clench the copper ring.
Muffled squeals escape the jaws

Clamped tight by ringer's hand.
There is a small bleed of bright blood.
The incontinence of fear
Thickens the air.
The ringer throws the pig aside.
Another is caught.

Cowed, tails straight,
The young pigs shake their heads,
Shiver in a corner, noses together,
Like the wheel-hub of a cart.

Tomorrow, they'll tear the silence apart
Again. Next week,
Castration.

This is a poem where alliteration, repetition and certain rhymes mingle. This in turn produces internal rhythms that help to create atmosphere, as much as the careful selection of words and effective use of vowels.

We have seen in previous chapters how rhythm can be created by the metrical pattern of a poem. It is often best, to establish the metrical pattern by ear, to let the natural speech patterns of stressed and unstressed syllables lead into the discovery of a metre best suited for the poem being written.

If metre is not used, and free verse is the medium for the poem, then check the lineation frequently. Also note the pauses, this includes allowing time for a particular thought to be emphasised, so that a reader may respond to the same thought. The pause may simply be one that is required for a breathing space, and can be made obvious to readers by a punctuation mark, a dash, or a blank space between words, lines or stanzas.

It can be the music of a poem that enhances its underlying message, and the most commonly used mediums to set up internal melody are the metrical and rhyming patterns.

The most frequently used rhyming pattern, or so it seems from the poems that students hand to me, are the rhymes used on line endings. These help make good expressive poetry, but it is surprising the number of people writing poetry who are convinced that they are not writing it correctly if their work does not rhyme.

Because of this, and the concern it brings, they often rush their selection of rhyming words, and totally lose the definition of the emotive quality in their work. There is also a tendency to lose the rhyme as the poem progresses. For example, a poem may start off with a rhyming pattern like this:

The room was square and small
A man's huge frame a part of it,
The dog lay gazing at the hall
Moving only as the lamp was lit.

Note the rhyming pattern:

1st line:	(a)
2nd line:	(b)
3rd line:	(a)
4th line:	(b)

As the story in the poem develops, the tendency is to work more rapidly and the rhyme can become mislaid, as can be seen in the second stanza of the same poem:

The man arose, his chair creaked back	(a)
He stood beside his dog	(b)
The lamplight formed huge shadows	(c)
And the fire sputtered on a log.	(b)

We are certainly getting the storyline, and at a cracking pace, but suddenly the rhyming pattern has changed to that of: a b c b. Obviously the rhythm has changed as well, and although we have only analysed the rhyme pattern the poet must pay equal attention to rhythm.

The poet who wrote these lines was intensely concerned with the unfolding drama, but there must be organisation to arrange the correct proportions of rhyme and rhythm in a poem.

If the difference in rhyme in the second stanza has achieved a certain good effect, perhaps emphasised tension or atmosphere, then the poet would know that this pattern would be the best medium to work in, and consequently arrange any other stanza in the same way.

Here and there in this chapter it has been suggested that poems are analysed to see how they work and what gives them their appeal to readers. To do this, ask yourself whether the basic idea in the poem is established in a way that is under-stated, or whether it is projected or portrayed flamboyantly. Perhaps the meaning is emphasised in a satirical way? This will be discovered if a poem is read thoughtfully, line by line. Ask yourself when reading a poem whether the poet uses rhyme or rhythm to interpret ideas? If so, do these have a gentle tone, a musical background or a full orchestral accompaniment? For example, the heroic couplet is one method of exposing folly, or a human error, and holding it up to ridicule. Every line, in this type of poem, rhymes with its adjacent lines, and may contain any selected number of such couplets.

When writing a poem the poet must ask where, when or why, the poem reaches the heights intended. Or whether it fails as a piece of work that is intended to fascinate, persuade, or emotionally move a reader in some way.

From analytical criticism something will be learned about techniques, and how to use them, for they are not artificial props as much as essential aids to writing poetry. To analyse does not mean continually to find fault. It means to assess and hopefully find something in a poem that surprises, delights and evokes a response. One cannot be ignorant of technicalities and still be able to pass fair comments, even on one's own work. As an aid to the writing of rhymed poetry, certain patterns coded by letters of the alphabet are listed on the following page. Possibly, when writing your own poems, instead of using this well tried method, you will be able to invent ways which will help retain the idea of a regular rhyming sequence. It will be seen that quite logically, as rhymes and lines change, that the alphabet patterning is also changed:

1. line rhyming: (a)
2. line unrhymed: (b)
3. line rhyming: (a)
4. line unrhymed: (b)

This pattern may, as the poem progresses during composition, be changed to a pattern of: a b b a. Here is an example:

A boy runs with his dog and kite (a)
lifts his face to the sky (b)
knows only truth, and no lie (b)
at this moment of gold and blue light (a)

It can be heard, if the stanza is read aloud, that the rhyme is not making the right music. We judge this by our auditory sense, and it is usually quite an instinctive choice at first whether the rhyme chosen fits the image.

In this instance, it is the soft sound of the letter *l* on the last word *light* that defeats the pattern. The emphasis of *kite* is inclined towards the hard *k* sound. Almost subconsciously, we wait for the same emphasis on the word *light*, especially as the eye sees it as the last word of the last line, and the voice drops in recognition of this fact.

Let us try the stanza in another way:

Running with his dog and kite, a boy (a)
lifts his face to the sky (b)
knows only truth and no lie (b)
at this moment of gold and blue joy (a)

This works better, and the rhymes are still structured in the same pattern. It may work even better if we try it another way:

Running with his dog and kite, a boy (a)
lifts his face to the sky (b)
at this moment of gold and blue joy (a)
knows only truth and no lie (b)

The sound, through the pattern of rhyme, has been changed and the lines run off the tongue more easily. Remember, it is the sounds within a poem that help to convey the meaning.

'Look at birthday, or anniversary cards, they have verses that rhyme don't they?' That was a cry from the heart of a group of my creative writing students. They had been to a reading by a well known poet. The poet wrote in contemporary style, and it was good. Unfortunately, some of my group had (in their own words) 'been unable to connect with the subject matter,' simply because the poetry did not rhyme.

There will, of course, always be personal preferences just as there are in any other art forms. We each of us know what we like. Why do we like whatever it is? Mainly because it appeals to us in some way that is peculiar to our own sensitivity and sensibility.

It is sometimes argued that intelligence is a secondary thing, and that instinct is the guiding factor. We hang a picture on a wall because it relaxes or intrigues, or simply makes us feel happy. We like its colours, we may even feel the same about a piece of sculpture we have bought, something that everyone else pulls a face at.

It is the same with poetry. We like a poem because we respond to it in some way. If we hear a poem read aloud, then we will respond to it because of the way it is read, 'and if it rhymes,' my group argued, 'then we will anticipate or respond to the poem more keenly.' It was the line ending rhymes that they missed. This group felt strongly that such rhymes helped to convey a meaning within a poem. The rhythm, they said, lulls a listener into a poem. This is certainly a valid point but if a poem is well written, using the devices that go to make up rhythm and rhyme other than those used on line endings, then its music will still be heard.

A defined rhyme, whether on line endings, or within the structure of a poem will, if it is placed correctly, clinch the effect that the poem aims for. Emotion and atmosphere can be emphasised by the carefully thought out rhymes.

It may be true that intellect takes its place after instinct when creating a poem, but this does not mean that a poem should not be revised in an intelligent way. Certain stress patterns as well as the use of carefully selected consonants and vowels, will direct how a poem is to be presented. Emotions can be poured into a rush of words, or a mood established by letting words flow easily into a certain pace. Rhymes and the rhythms of speech bring a musical quality to poems.

Without rhythm, the ideas and intentions in poetic thought will not be so prominent as they should be. Think of the incantations of tribal rhythms, or the lines of a poem or song that compel because they come with regularity. One only has to see a magpie in a garden and the well known chant, probably learned in our formative years, springs to mind:

One for sorrow
Two for mirth
Three for a wedding
Four for a birth...

Rhymes have, as we have seen in this chapter, had algebraic codes put on them, and rhythms have similar labels. It is important to remember that both rhythm and rhyme can emphasise the intensity of feeling in poetry. It is for this reason that they need to be thought about carefully.

Rhymes and rhythms combined in a poem reinforce the depth of thought that went into writing it. For example, the traditional patterns of these two things can be savoured in the following sonnet:

Sussex Drought by B. Cross

Land lies corn-drowsy in the summer heat,
Poppy-somnolent, indolent, stretched out
To parched horizons. Deepening drought
Colours the earth ash-grey, to stain the feet
Of sandalled walkers. Insects secrete,
Seduce and tantalise; the chrysalis clout
Cast for the butterfly, the rouseabout –
The grasshopper – with rock-musician beat
Pervades the fields. Ditches are dust-dry.

Across the sky a single vapour trail
Whitens cerulean blue. Trees sigh
And sough in a brief, blessed breeze. Bale
After bale of hay is shaped to lie
In parcels. Sun is a pitiless flail.

Poets have the choice of using rhyme and rhythm in traditional or contemporary forms of poetry. They should be well thought out and controlled. If rhythms are too contrived they will merely show that a poet does not know how to use them subtly; if rhymes are not carefully chosen, they will appear as an affectation.

Handled well, rhymes and rhythms can greatly assist the music, the message and the inner depth of a poem.

11
Imagery

How is imagery achieved in a poem? One way is by effective use of language, which persuades readers and listeners to see something concrete. For example in the following lines the image is made to appear real. It is the language of poetry, a metaphorical language:

My mother rolled rather than walked,
a comfortable, eiderdown sort of woman,
with soft folds, and tucks that comforted.

The image is made more real than if the lines are written as:

My mother was round shaped, warm and cuddly.

It is the eiderdown image that gives an effective description of a comforting mother with 'soft folds, and tucks that comforted.' This image makes us look at this familiar object in a different way. It amuses, surprises, and produces a certain picture in our minds. This is what poetry is all about, it sets out to evoke a response of some sort in readers. Poets attempt to achieve this by a number of ways, including the use of imagery.

One of the poet's tasks is to help their readers see familiar things in different, more unusual ways. Pure description can create an image as for example in:

Small stones like beads

This is a fair description and is also a simile – something where the comparison of objects is made explicit by the link words *like* and *as*.

If this particular simile is elaborated, the image can be made more forceful:

Small stones, a scattered rosary

The small stones were not of course a rosary, but the image has been described through the use of metaphor, and metaphor is the application of a word to something that it does not apply to literally. So the 'small beads' have become a 'scattered rosary'.

This is an obvious example and you can, as an exercise, list a number of items in metaphoric form, trying to make the metaphors as subtle as possible.

An image in a poem can of course also be a symbol. The white dove of peace for example, or the red rose for love. A poppy, crucifix, snakes, dragons, all have been used as symbols in poetry.

If symbols are not used carefully, however, they can overload a poem with all reference to them becoming so obvious that the meaning of the poem is overlooked. Symbols can be selected carefully for pointers in a poem, or placed throughout it in such a way that they reinforce the main theme.

Images can grasp the reader intellectually; they can also filter through in a persuasive way into the sense interpretation of a reader. They can definitely bring an emotional jolt into the reading of a poem.

Among the poems that achieve this is Sylvia Plath's *The Rabbit Catcher* in which imagery is sustained throughout.

In the first stanza of this poem, the reader becomes aware of something ominous, a sense of impending doom. Sylvia Plath describes the elements as though they are her foes: the sea holds death, the wind torments her viciously. The poem leads step by step, and line by line, towards the snare. The killing of the rabbit is a metaphor for what is felt to be the destruction of a part of her own life. The second stanza has images that dwell on this theme and the reader is pulled into the poem by the fear that is evoked through these images.

This poet is daring in the highly original choice of words. The 'malignity of the gorse' for example. Below are five lines from the second stanza:

I tasted the malignity of the gorse,
Its black spikes,
The extreme unction of its yellow candle-flowers.
They had an efficiency, a great beauty,
And were extravagant, like torture.

The *black spikes* sound lethal, the image is one of terror, and the *extreme unction* brings the hour of death to mind – the rite of anointing a dying person with oil. The flowers referred to have *a great beauty*, but it is a beauty that is *extravagant*, it is too much, *like torture*.

It is not merely the pictorial images that evoke a response, it is also the sounds of the words. For instance, the two hard *g*'s in line one of the above stanza plus the hard *k*'s in the second line emphasise the starkness of the image. The spikes are black, the readers response is to associate them with pain, and even death.

The rhythm in the poem is precise, compelling you to read it in the way the poet intended. The language and imagery is powerful, and we identify with the emotions that the poet is writing of.

Poets attempt to draw readers into the impressions they themselves have received from certain experiences, although to attempt this is not an easy task. Pictorial images, and selective use of words and phrases, can help achieve this by suggesting ideas through their vividness, overtones of mystery, and emotional depth.

Imagery makes a poet stretch the muscles of the mind. For example, if rain is simply described as *falling*, and even if the description is broadened to *delicately falling*, an image is still not being created. However, if the rain is described as *falling needle like*, the description moves closer to imagery.

Imagery can intensify the emotive quality of poetry as in the following four lines from a Shakespeare sonnet describing the ageing process:

When forty winters shall besiege thy brow
And dig deep trenches in thy beauty's field,
Thy youth's proud livery, so gazed on now,
Will be a tattered weed, of small worth held:

How much more emotive this description is than it would have been had the words merely spoken of *wrinkles* or *lines* on a face.

It is possible to see from the examples in this chapter that several things are involved in creating imagery. Obviously, a careful selection of words is important – just as it is in all aspects of writing.

The poet endeavours to draw readers directly into the poem, placing them right in the scene or story (or both). An image creates a mental picture, and this process involves all the senses as you will see them from the following:

Visual Imagery: An illustration of this is 'Sunflowers spilling from yellow pots along the dressers edge/and purple tulips like hanging lamps, bordering the window ledge.'
Aural Imagery: 'The lamb repeats the plea in its throat/juddering cold air.'
Olfactory Imagery: 'Mother grew primroses, lilies and herbs,/wound through our yard a fragrance from childhood/and the honeysuckle trailing a green archway trellis,/evoked the same memories.'
Gustatory Imagery: 'And seaspray like tears, tastes salt in my memory.'
Tactile Imagery: 'As gentle-fingered he firmed a root, or reaching up beyond his head, felt in the vine for globuled fruit.'
Kinetic Imagery: 'He communicates by signs/and rustles bank notes.'

Hyperbole, another of those long sounding words, means an exaggerated statement that is not meant to be taken literally (such as: It is raining cats and dogs). This device can also be used in imagery, and can be very emphatic.

Repetition can shape imagery in a poem, and an illustration of this is in the following extract:

Celebration by L. Richardson

Eight magpies came to my garden
Eight Astaires looking for their silver-headed sticks
Eight clacking vandals savaging the crabs
Eight fops searching for their toppers
Eight lugubrious widowers in half-mourning
Eight praying prelates free from their prayers
Eight paper boys with hands in pockets
Eight rooks self-consciously in fancy dress

Imagery, as we have seen in the examples, can be emphatic but it can also be implied gently. In his poem *Ode To Autumn*, John Keats presents us with a tranquil scene, the imagery simply implies that the poem is about Autumn. He draws his readers through the sights, sounds and sensations of Autumn:

Where are the songs of Spring? Ay, where are they?
Think not of them, thou hast thy music too, –
While barrèd clouds bloom the soft-dying day,
And touch the stubble-plains with rosy hue;
Then in a wailful choir the small gnats mourn
Among the river sallows, borne aloft
Or sinking as the light wind lives or dies;
And full-grown lambs loud bleat from hilly bourn;
Hedge-crickets sing; and now with treble soft
The redbreast whistles from a garden-croft;
And gathering swallows twitter in the skies.

By inference, imagery, rhyme and rhythm, a picture of Autumn is presented in this stanza. The imagery used is subtle, but is nevertheless a tremendous reinforcement of what the poem is saying.

Poets try to communicate their own feelings in their

poems, and at the time of writing these may be intense. It is partly through the imagery they use that they enable readers to identify with the emotions and feelings they are expressing. Imagery does not always have to be used flamboyantly; it does not have to use repetitive expressions, nor sensuous descriptive stanzas. It can be used in a restrained way, and one excellent example of restrained yet powerful imagery is in the following few lines from *Autobiography* by Louis MacNeice. The knowledge that this poet's mother died when he was five years old, makes the restrained emotion appear even more highly charged:

> *My mother wore a yellow dress;*
> *Gently, gently, gentleness.*
>
> *Come back early or never come.*
>
> *When I was five the black dreams came;*

By the use of soft sounds (as in the letter *s*) and by repetition of certain words, and through the lyrical quality of the whole poem, the image presents the emotional sense contained within the words.

At times, the imagery used in words and phrases seems to arise instinctively. Imagery can be analysed and discussed, yet the magic it evokes does not require any explanation.

Imagery can clarify and intensify the depth of emotion within poems. In this way, the object or experience that the poet is presenting is made vivid, and its impact is felt by readers.

In the examples that have been given in this chapter it can be seen that imagery can be used in many ways. This depends, of course, on the subject matter, the tone of the poem, and the style that the poet adopts.

Let us take the idea of tone first of all, for it is the tone that helps to define the overall sense. The tone of nostalgia, for example, can be produced by summoning up a glimpse, or several glimpses, of an image or images from the past:

A Room Remembered

This room is crowded out
with memories.

The armchair that had always
been side-edged, into the gap
between the fire and dresser shelves.

The table spread for welcoming,
linen cloth touched with lace. The gentle,
assured acceptance of my place,

the scent of hyacinths, neat, orderly
array of teacups upon the tray.

Invisible, the cord that binds me here,
where hollow emptiness now echoes
on the wooden floor.

Cat-cradled in the cord's silk threads,
I am entangled in the past;

my thoughts are drawn into the room
beyond the hall. I cannot reconcile
such emptiness with love,

where now the fire is dead
and dust cascades from crumbling walls.

Let us now think about another issue involved, that of style. In the poem given as an example below, the poet uses imagery throughout the poem, and from the first line it makes an impact on the reader:

Feet First by B. Whincup

The puff – and huff – that flew
my kite above the spring-rising
high, ghosts the glass
with a smudge, that is just

big enough to obscure
the passing glance of summer

now the wild green water flooding
her veins evaporates,
in the brood and blaze of autumn.

And it's in the confines
of the withering wood – where
improbable spaces hold
still the twitch of the pinch and
pulse of passion – that the
winter-seeded snowdrops sleep
but must, all too soon, awake

to wreathe a shovelful of earth.

It is a poem where the images come thick and fast, and the poet's style makes readers constantly aware of the deeper meaning within the poem. We chase the images along each line, the pace of the poem directing this.

What imagery does in a poem, amongst other things, is to help suggest the poem's literal meaning. It does this by evoking the sense of the meaning underlying the poem. That might sound complicated, but it is how poetry works, and it is part of the magic that we expect it to have. A poem that uses imagery is usually more emotively effective than if statement and pure description were dominating each stanza.

The composers of music set out to envelop our senses with their personal interpretation of something, while the painter uses colour to bring an impression to our senses. The poet tries to relate the sense of a particular experience through words, and more often than not succeeds. A momentary but sharp perception may have brought the poem into existence. By highlighting this particular moment through imagery, the poet can evoke the senses and understanding of readers. Each poet has his or her own voice, and this within their poetry makes them unique.

Imagery does not replace imagination. Rather the imaginative thought process is brought into play through its use. The first image that comes to mind may bring the sharp perception of a poem, on the other hand it may bring something that appears to be slightly out of focus. This may be because the idea presenting itself is forming through a series of images which, although to begin with, may seem a little confused, will eventually define the emotive quality of a poem.

If a particular sentiment is expressed in a poem, the use of imagery can support it. Poetry written without imagery often proves to be little more than pure statement. Without imagery the metaphorical language of poetry can be forgotten. The following written by a student is an example:

Waiting for a length of time
Watching the sand in the hour glass
Evaporate, like hope.

These few lines, do not have the flourish of poetry, although there has been an attempt to include an image in the three lines. Obviously the student intended there to be a certain connection between the image of the hour glass and of hope.

These few lines were not written in a moment of perception, they were part of an exercise in poetry, and as they stand would not remain long in the minds of readers, either as an emphatic statement or a worthy image to surround the underlying meaning in the lines. The image does not work, and sand does not evaporate although, metaphorically, hope might. The image would have to be rewritten to be effective, and this is where revision serves a useful purpose.

The best lines of poetry often include imagery that has come through the instinctive ideas of the poet. Imagery is one factor in making the readers or listeners draw on their own powers of perception. If the poet uses imagery selectively and skilfully, the meaning and depth of a poem will be fully appreciated. The reader will, if the images are strong enough, put the correct connection on them, so that what they imply will enhance the message, meaning and beauty within a poem.

After the following poem you will find a number of questions are listed; the imagery within the poem should spark off your answers:

Chernobyl

This should have been a springtime
morning;
unprepared, we waited
for shadows to shroud the sky,
our dreams turning ash-grey.

This should have been a springtime
morning;
not a day filled
with the ominous silence
of our fears,

not a beginning
with the salt taste of tears
in our mouths,

and the priest's wafer
crumbling
into the acrid dust;

the tears of our unborn
destroy us, too late to savour
Spring, or watch for the returning swallows.

Question 1: What is meant by the lines in the last stanza: *the tears of our unborn destroy us*?
Question 2: What does the reference to *swallows* in the last line refer to?

Exercise 1: Think of any emotive effect this poem may have had on you (such as fear, unease, uncertainty, depression). Make a list of the emotions you experienced when reading the poem or afterwards.
Exercise 2: Write a poem in which you use imagery to communicate one of the emotions you have listed. At first

using a series of connecting images through the poem, these should relate to your emotion in some way.
Exercise 3: Write a poem using an image as the title, and bring this title into the poem at some point as a reinforcement.

The answers to the questions are:
Answer 1: The effects of radiation carry through to other generations, and unborn children suffer.
Answer 2: Swallows migrate and their return is associated with the beginning of summer. The reference to them in the poem implies that the natural world is now chaotic, or that some of those who were present during the Chernobyl disaster may not live to see the swallows returning.

By the use of imagery, poets persuade readers to draw on their imaginative resources and to find inner depths of meaning.

It has been discussed in this chapter how to create and establish imagery in poems. This can, as we have seen, be done by the use of pictorial images. Rhythm is also a factor in arousing the emotions of readers, and creating tensions within lines of a poem. If sounds are strongly patterned within lines, attention will be drawn to these. For example, in *Gulls call across cliffs, like cries of grief* we can hear, if the line is read aloud, how the emphasis on the hard sound of the letter *c* with back-up from the letters *g* has slowed the pace of the poem. If tensions were being built within the framework, this slow pace could be continued into the next lines of the poem.

It can be noted in the following lines written by a schoolgirl aged eight, that the child is reinforcing each sound quite instinctively, allowing the developing pattern to lead her into the choice of words. The poem is called *Fireworks* and her opening lines are:

Crack and snap and twizzle
and dazzle,

Crack, snap and crash!

The girl has made the sounds of the words resemble the image of the outline of her poem, as yet unfinished.

Imagery in this way is formed through onomatopoeia, the words imitating or suggesting what they stand for.

If the overall theme of a poem is a gentle one, then the pace can be easy, and words selected that are of a gentle quality, as for example:

slumber sweetly, still and silent…

Tension would not be required in this type of poem, so a steady measure of rhythm within the lines would be suitable. And language selected to enhance this gentle quality might be something on the lines of the following:

your eyelids, like flower petals, closed

This way, an image is being formed.

Imagery can, as we have seen in this chapter clarify with great intensity the subject matter of a poem. It should never be overlooked as a worthy aid by anyone writing poetry.

12
Punctuation, Pace And Other Matters

There are several things that go into the creation of a good poem. Imagery, metre, rhyme and forms have been discussed in previous chapters. Explanations of why and how these devices are used have been given. One of the best ways to learn about poetry is to read a great deal of it, then write some of your own, using devices that assist your poems in some way.

Punctuation should not be overlooked. It may seem an insignificant matter, but it has great importance in poetry. A poem is a work of art, something that will hopefully be read and heard by many. What the poet sets out to achieve, therefore, has to be as near perfection as possible.

Punctuation in the following few lines is necessary for breath control, and without it the phrases and lines would merge together:

Winter has come, stealthily in the night
across cracked paving stones. Frost glints coldly
in early light; the air cuts clean
and all the holly boughs hang heavy under snow.

The pause at the word *light* is required not merely to take a breath, but to emphasise the rhyme, while the full stop after *stones* divides the images.

A stanza from a poem written in sprung rhythm by Gerard Manley Hopkins, who devised this method of music in poetry, shows the importance of punctuation.

Hurrahing In Harvest

I walk, I lift up heart, eyes,
Down all that glory in the heavens to glean our Saviour;
And, eyes, heart, what looks, what lips yet gave you a
Rapturous love's greeting of realer, of rounder replies?

Read the lines aloud and note how the punctuation matters to the rhythm, particularly the effective pauses after the commas. Careful thought has obviously gone into the placing of the semi-colon at the end of the second line. This enhances the distinctly reverent pause which brings a reflective quality to this line.

As always, the poet has a choice where to use punctuation: perhaps within lines, at the end of them, or possibly not at all. From the examples quoted it can be seen that punctuation can help to define the rhythm within a poem. Obviously, full stops and commas can bring significant as well as minute breath pauses. Question marks are important, and exclamation marks can give added power and punch to lines within a poem.

Words, phrases and lines as well controlled as those in the poem set out below, do not need the additional emphasis of punctuation marks:

In My Dreamfield by A. Bielski

you have felled an oak in my dreamfield
I was going to walk there tonight
over emerald grass

you have found my secret place
lonely moon balanced on leaves
and those pallid flowers
brushing my knees with shadows

who said you could enter my dreamfield?
it is private property
you have spoilt it with clumsiness

I built it up blade by blade
leaf by favourite leaf
discovered shade widened a stream
built a seat under branches

it was my refuge
rustling at night with special sounds
and undiscovered stars

now that tree is a nightmare
with limbs wrenched into ugly angles
and useless naked roots
I tried to burn it

but only its bark blackened
it lies there a solid monument
breaking contours of sleep

and nothing is the same
my silver leaves are all tarnished
the stream muddy with wakened clay
I shall have to find a new place

for even my dreams are vulnerable
you always come into them
I shall have to take you with me to living fields

The music and meaning is enhanced as well as controlled in the poem by a disciplined approach to sound and line breaks. Vowel patterning and the use of alliteration, as well as slight rhymes and echoes, lead readers into how the poem should be read. Without punctuation, apart from that of the vital question mark on line eight, there are still pauses which occur strategically on the beat of a word or line.

If, however, a poem had been written in a defined rhyming pattern, one that had to be read at a fast pace, then without the necessary punctuation a reader would arrive quickly, and somewhat breathlessly at the last line. The following poem was written as an exercise at a children's workshop session:

The Ghost

I live in house that's very old
The floorboards creak and groan
The windows rattle in the night
And I'm scared to be alone

They say an old man haunts the place
And shouts out in the night
I only know that if he does
I'll simply die of fright

The door frame rattles and the door
The lamps keep going flicker
They say this ghost can really run
But I shall run much quicker

They say he comes behind you
In the night-time when it's black
He sends a shiver up your spine
And taps upon your back

I'm told you never see him
But hear him breathing there
I only know that if I do
I'll crawl beneath a chair

The most obvious punctuation mark that has been omitted is the exclamation mark at the end of the poem. Although the words and rhythm are straightforward, pauses are required, both for effect as much as for breath control. The voice needs to drop at the end of the second stanza, so that a reader has a definite pause for dramatic effect before the start of the third stanza 'The door frame rattles...' Several small pauses are required in various lines of the poem. For instance, a full stop at the end of the third stanza, or possibly an exclamation mark here for emphasis. A comma placed at the end of the second line in the final stanza would build up the drama and tension in its last two lines.

It is always best to read aloud any poem that you are

working on. The punctuation can often be overlooked in the heat of finding the right words, form and rhythm. If the poem reads well, and the necessary pauses are obvious, then leave the poem for a few days before returning to it and reading it aloud yet again.

It should now become apparent where pauses and line breaks should occur. Check to see if these are sufficient, note if line breaks should be changed. Line breaks, or lines where the break or pause coincides with a unit of meaning, are very important in showing how the poem should be read. Enjambment, which is when the sense of one stanza line is run on into the next line without pause, is often used in both traditional and free verse.

The eyes and the ears of readers will understand the relevance of enjambment. When a poem has lines that run over into others, the pauses will seem to be achieved naturally. This device was introduced at some point over the years as poets grew tired of what they considered a too deliberate method of effecting a pause. The subtle use of enjambment can add emphasis to the phrase being read, and the sense of the initial line can be taken up in the ones that follow. Here is an example of enjambment:

And early on the cock was heard to crow
not once, but twice
and then again, and we shivered in our souls.

The idea is to take the reader by surprise, and often means that enjambment creates a pause for effect. If used too often, however, this device will prove very monotonous and its power will be limited.

Devices, including the use of punctuation (or non-use of it) are used, or they should be used, to evoke sense impressions and to engage a reader's attention. If, however, devices like enjambment are used merely as affectations, then they do nothing to enhance a poem.

The opposite to enjambment is the line that is termed as being end-stopped. The pauses created by both enjambment and line endings can be seen in the following poem:

As a Child

As a child when visiting, I held the snapshot,
soldier image in its frame, it showed a laughing man,
not then, the half-hidden terror
in his eyes, as war gas choked and wreathed
around his lungs.

He'd reach across the space between and grip
my hand, each breath a triumph every day
against the pungency of gas, that once had crept
inside his army uniform and mask.

Death made a noisy entrance in the room,
it tore and rattled at his throat. I was ushered out,
and waiting in the hallway's lincrusta gloom
I heard the sounds diminish – sigh
to silence – when at last the cavern of my uncle's mouth
became a round, perpetual gasp.

When reading poetry, not only your own but that written by others, stop when you come to what appears to be a natural pause. Think why the pause is effective at this point. What has been achieved? When you are writing poetry take note where you feel a comma or full stop is required. At first, when forming the outline of a poem you will do whatever comes naturally. Reading your poem aloud afterwards will help you decide whether a full stop at the end of a line is what is required, or whether the rove-over style of enjambment would be suitable instead. It is likely that your initial pauses, marked by some sort of punctuation, were there because you drew breath at those particular points in the poem. During a revision period, and revision is discussed in another chapter, you will be able to decide if the punctuation marks you have used have any particular relevance to the sense of the poem. Let us just rehearse some of the basic principles of punctuation in poetry:

The full stop: Used as an indication of where to end a sentence, or a line of thought.

The comma: Used not only to indicate a pause but also to prevent readers from connecting words that do not belong together. It is useful when placed between adjectives, as in for example: It was a large, dirty room. It is well used in separating items in sentences, and on lists. It is often essential to use a comma in lines of poetry.

In the following example a number of punctuation marks are used, and they were considered essential when writing the poem:

Let us sister, hurry then,
Now ! Arise! Come away!
To the distant moors and crags,
And the rocks and mossy paths
Where summer rain has left is mark,
And the sky is imaged in a pool.

Let us consider why the punctuation marks in these lines were considered by the poet to be essential. Firstly, the exclamation marks are used to bring a sense of urgency to the second line. They emphasise the fact that someone is being urged to 'arise and come away'. The commas are useful as breath pauses, they also slow the tempo a little, as in the first line for instance. If this had been written without the commas ('Let us sister hurry then') the music introduced in this line would seem entirely different. The comma helps to keep the pace steady and carefully measured. Without it, the whole line would seem out of rhythm with the rest of the stanza, rather like trying to dance the quickstep when it is waltz time that is being played.

The semi-colon: A useful mark when a pause is required that is somewhat longer than a comma, but not so long as a full stop. Again, reading a poem aloud as it is being composed will denote whether a line requires a comma, full stop, or semi-colon.

The colon: Often the best mark to use when a pause significantly longer than that of the semi-colon is required.

Exclamation marks: These can often be overused, and care should be taken when writing a poem to make sure that their use is justified.

The apostrophe: A punctuation mark that is often overlooked, and sometimes omitted in lines of poetry. An apostrophe, of course, has several uses such as to show when a letter (or letters) has been omitted from a word, for example in *don't* instead of *do not* and *'phone* instead of *telephone*. It can also indicate possession as in: That is my son's coat.
Speech marks: Used to indicate dialogue.
Dash: Often used when an additional phrase or word is placed in a line which is grammatically complete without it, as in: I went to the window – I had been on the other side of the room – which overlooked the street.

A dash may also be used to illustrate an abrupt change of thought, as in: I will take you – but no, you would not come.

A dash can be used where the poet thinks that a number of commas may make a line look overloaded as in:

long Sunday mornings with the papers read –
in the kitchen – windows steaming

The image within these lines is summed up, and it appears that the use of the dash has gathered together all the necessary components to achieve this.
A hyphen: Can prevent ambiguity, as for example in: A blue-and-white tray. This implies that the tray is composed of two colours rather than writing 'a blue and white tray' which could imply that there is a blue tray and a white one. Hyphens are also used to join two words together, as in *picture-postcard* or *tree-top*.
Punctuation is something often used instinctively, and its hardly thought about as being one of the more useful poetic devices. It can however help to control the poem, encompassing both line units and the music. Sometimes it is discarded by contemporary poets who may feel that a poem stands on its own assets of language and imagery, and that pauses will develop naturally if the poem is laid out in a given way. It is, however, much more difficult to control a poem without the use of punctuation, and to have to rely on other methods to control its pace.
Capital letters: It was once considered the rule to start each

line of poetry with a capital letter but, as with so many other rules, this is no longer slavishly applied. The use of capital letters can be rejected altogether if the poet believes this will help the poem. Capital letters, even if they are not preceded by a full stop can be used to highlight a word that the poet wishes to draw attention to.

The pace of a poem is something that punctuation, as well as the device of enjambment, can help to control. Poems naturally vary in their pace depending on the subject matter, those that resemble songs will, for example, have a different pace from those aiming at a more conversational tone.

If after writing a poem, or even after writing its first few stanzas, its pace appears to be dragging, check how many words with long syllables have been used because these will tend to slow the pace. A slow pace can be made faster by using a less restrictive rhythm, enjambing more lines, or by using words and phrases that suggest quickness of movement.

A poem that is going along at a cracking pace is fine – if it is meant to do so. The following lines, for example, unfold a story that requires this pace:

I met a shy young girl
Seventeen, or so she said.
Her hair was inclined to curl
In ringlets round her head.

The sing-song pace can be heard in these opening four lines, and if the poem is following a narrative style then this sing-song effect may well be suitable. But if the poem develops away from the narrative style, then the poet would need to lose the rhymes, or at least this particular rhyming pattern. A rhyming pattern that would be less obtrusive and which would slacken the pace could work like this:

I met a shy young maiden
Seventeen, or so she said
Her hair was gold and bright
In ringlets round her head.

Try to be aware of the pace of each line of any poem that you write. As an exercise, try using only four words on the first line of a stanza, each word to consist of only one syllable. Then in the second line, use six words, but making sure that one of them consists of three syllables. Vary the number of words in the next line, say perhaps five, with one of them having at least three syllables. Make the last line of the stanza consist of eight words, and be sure to make at least two of these have two syllables.

Write at least two more stanzas in this way. Vary the syllables and the pace, and add rhyme or omit it, as you require. Rhyme will change the pace of your poem depending on the pattern used.

When using the syllable count exercise as a way of controlling your pace you will find that eight or ten syllables in each line will produce the regular rhythm of the iambic tetrameter and pentameter patterns (see chapter four).

Take careful note of the stress patterns in speech when writing poems, for these can advance or slow down the pace of lines. Syllable counts, whilst not always conforming to the accented metrical sequences, will be suitable for the requirements of a poem that seems to ponder on things in a fairly relaxed way. Note the measured pace of a Shakespearean or Petrarchan sonnet, as illustrated in chapter five, and try to define how this is achieved. Is it accomplished by the use of metrical patterns, or selective use of language? Do read a great deal of poetry, and examine the poems written in traditional and contemporary styles. Read them aloud and note how the pace is maintained, or changed, according to the poet's methods.

The plan within this chapter is to discuss the small but invaluable things that go into the creation of a good poem. A good poem means one where the poet has done the best with language and other devices that have already been mentioned in this and other chapters. It is rare for a complete poem to come to mind, without a great deal of thought and hard work an idea will get no further than a quick interpretation of basic thought.

Tone

If, after writing a poem, you wonder why it does not evoke the original feeling that drove you to write it, then read it aloud carefully. Check whether the feeling you had – whether of joy, fear, indignation, sorrow, or whatever – is encountered anywhere in the lines of your poem.

If it is not, then think about what has restricted the pouring out of such feelings. Did you restrict them by using too rigid a rhyming pattern? Of were your images unrelated to the strength of emotion you wished to convey? Perhaps the pace was too fast, or the tone too jocular, for the type of poem you intended to write? The tone of the poem will be conveyed through the choice of language, as well as the many devices at the poet's disposal that can help convey in subtle, or strident ways, the depth of emotion that is the inner depth of the poem.

For instance in the following sentences, the tone can be easily defined:

'You can't cook?'

'You are not my master!'

'I hate the sound of that squeaking door.'

If you were asked to describe the emotion conveyed in each of these lines you could do so in a few words. The meaning in each line is plain enough, and the tone within the words indicates the meaning. It is the voice that the poet displays that conveys mood and tone to a reader.

Novelists portray through their characters the depth of feeling within a given situation. Poets attempt to convey tone and mood through inference and imagery. The following is the start of a poem begun during a group session at a poetry workshop. The sensation of 'fear' had to be placed within eight lines, and this is what the group managed in a short space of time:

The Soldier

The noise was too much, the bullets and sighs,
unending cries, and all the while
he thought of home, the warmth of it
the bright lights, the prettiness of women
market places, rivers. He could see it, smell it,
knew it was warping his senses as he lay crying
and dying in the mud, rain and slush –
knew only death could bring some kind of hush.

During the discussion following the workshop session it was decided that the mood and tone of these lines could be one of regret, of a sense of loss rather than fear. This is an exercise to be recommended when trying to establish the tone of a poem.

Tenses

It is easy to shift tenses in a poem, especially in the first stage of writing it. A story, or an event, can be written about as if part of what is being described took place in the past and another part in the present. If not handled carefully, however, these movements in tense will assume the appearance of having been written by mistake. A definite division has to be shown between the tenses. The point of their being in the poem at all must be to achieve something and establish something in a reader's mind, as in this example:

I sit here in the small room
while he waits outside, for a while he waits;
I see his shadowy figure move from the leather chair
stand for a moment,
half turn towards the glass panelled door
through which I stare...
He walks away.

These lines began to circle around my brain one evening and, in that strange way that all poets know, the last line kept coming from nowhere. It seemed at the time that it just had to be those three words *He walks away* written in the present tense, as is the rest of the poem.

Up to that point, when reaching those final lines, the poem had moved along fairly easily. Later, during that same evening, something compelled me to return to the poem, and to change the tense in that line. The rhythm seemed more defined by the lengthening of the word *walks* to *walked*, and certainly the impact of the line and its emotive content was made more emphatic by changing the present tense to the past tense of *He walked away*. The drama of the moment when the man actually walked away seemed more emphatic when related in the past tense. It made the episode seem to be more final, and heightened the emotive factor of the poem. The poem is still being worked on, and readers will eventually judge whether this stanza has set a scene emotively enough, and decide for themselves whether the shift from present to past tense in the last line works as it is meant to:

Hospital Visit

I sit here in the small room
while he waits outside, for a while he waits:
I see his shadowy figure move
from the leather chair, stand for a moment,
half turn towards the glass panelled door
through which I stare

He walked away…

It has been suggested many times in this book that, when composing poetry, it helps to read your work aloud. Listening to a poem simply hearing the words and their sounds makes a considerable difference to the interpretation. The variation of sound helps the emotive depth to be recognised. This has sometimes been referred to as the language becoming 'an echo to the sense'. Poets need to use all the resources at their disposal to convey this echo. An interplay of sounds is one method to achieve it, while the connotations of words and their phrasing is another.

Onomatopoeia

One of the best known methods to achieve sound effects in

poetry is the use of onomatopoeia, the deliberate use of words that imitate the sound they refer to. For instance, the *buzz* of a bee or the *sizzle* of an egg in a frying pan. A prizewinning poem written by Roger Elkin is an excellent example of onomatopoeic phrasing, especially the last line with its emotive meaning in the German words which translate as *Forget-me-not*. The sound of this word in German communicates to readers the sound of the whispering surf:

Omaha Beach by R. Elkin

Seagulls cry alert: Mine. Mine.
Wave after wave assaults the shoreline.
Polished shells push explosively through sand.

Crabs founder like grounded tanks, or move
Amphibious and armoured, sideways and back.

There are carapaces and skulls, limbs and bones
Where they've gone over the top.

Starfish surrender arms for the cross of Lorraine.

Above, the sky is forget-me-not blue.

And, beneath feet, the surf is whispering
Vergissmeinnicht.

It can be seen from this example, and others, that certain letters can create sound effects. For instance the letters *p* and *b* simulate small explosive noises; try saying *balloon* or *patriarch* aloud, and you will hear what is meant.

This explosive sound can be heard in the following lines from Alfred, Lord Tennyson's poem. The letter *b* is reinforced by the hard sound of the letter *k* in this example:

Break, break, break,
On thy cold gray stones, O Sea!

These examples use onomatopoeia to create sound echoes of

an image created within lines. it can be seen that taking care with a word selection entails much more than simply choosing certain words with which to describe an idea. Words, intended to be used as an onomatopoeic device, will often convey a 'sound sense' through the letters they contain. It is not necessary to get too intense about this, but it will be the impression that these particular words bring to a poem that lift it above the ordinary.

Hyperbole

This is a way to emphasise, or even exaggerate, an idea or a main point in a poem. Take the following example: His work is stacked up mountain high! This is an obvious exaggeration, but it does highlight the situation by its variation from the truth. Care has to be taken when using this device, as it can be difficult to use when trying to relay some expression of a particular emotion.

Overstatement and Understatement

Overstatement is a common fault, but one that can be rectified during the revision period. For instance an obvious overstatement has been used in the following lines:

heard him calling
after the man's retreating, cowardly back:
'Tell her to come!'

Retreating in the context of this poem implies cowardice. The line would have the same meaning if the word *cowardly* had been omitted. There is no room for unnecessary words in a poem. Everything you write should enhance the theme of your poem. As well as an overstatement when working on a poem, it is possible to overlook small unnecessary repetitions: the words *the* as well as *and* being the most commonly used small words that can be changed or left out.

Poetry requires subtlety. It is a strange thing, but the major point of a poem is made more obvious when it is merely inferred. To achieve this, some poets leave deliberate gaps between words so that readers will be intrigued and bring their own definition of the meaning, or understanding of an emotion, to the poem. An example is in the following lines:

As she lay resting amongst the flowers
her   skin   like the   outer petals
of a rose.

This method may not be to everyone's taste, and it may not be suited to the poem you are currently engaged in writing. It is however an innovation, an attempt to draw readers into the poem by persuading them to use their imaginations, and in this way to respond to what the poet is saying.

To use understatement is to place a deliberate restraint on the power within a poem. It can also, if used well, be a method of arousing dramatic tension. For example, in the following poem a lamb is being born:

Small Events

Thin, scratched lines
on the face of a dead moon,
screech of owl invades moorland silence
winged urgency vibrating like a small night wind.

The ewe, throb of insistence in her belly
shelters behind granite,
ice-capped lair of sabre-toothed
sullen land-mark, ironbound to earth.

A cloud drifts across
the moon,

the ewe shudders, a heaving dark mound.
Blood matting earth traces a shadow
beneath the pulsing wet of newborn lamb.

Dawn, not sudden, diffuses light
into a grey landscape,
spreads a recurring hope.

The lamb stumbles,
repeats the plea in its throat
juddering cold air,
and seeks familiar scents to suck vitality.

The original poem was purely a descriptive flow of how the lamb looked, and the scenery was referred to as a main part of the poem. My early efforts on this made me disconsolate until, encouraged by fellow poets, the theme of the whole piece was established as being that of 'hope'. Having accepted this, the next thing for me to do was to make this plain within the lines. The description of the colour of skies and moorland, the overall greyness of the landscape, all this had been repetitious and boring. The stanza containing all of this was cut to a mere three lines, and the change from greyness to light was shown by one word *diffuses*. The theme is now in this stanza – the fifth. The poem gained more strength from leaving out description of scenery and baring the lines down to words conveying images, as in: granite; ice-capped lair; moorland silence. Once the overstatement within the poem was sorted out the theme of hope became predominant.

Personification

The word says what it means: something, a non-living object, is treated as though it were living. An example of this can be seen in John Keats' *Ode to Autumn* where the second stanza refers to the season as a person:

Who hath not seen thee oft amid thy store?
Sometimes whoever seeks abroad may find
Thee sitting careless on a granary floor,
Thy hair soft-lifted by the winnowing wind;

Most of the devices mentioned in this book are often used quite unconsciously when writing poetry. The particular ones being discussed in this chapter do however, need to be considered carefully. It is possible to avoid overstatement in a poem, but does a poem work if its meaning is not made clear because it is understated? This can be checked during revision time. Onomatopoeic effects need careful planning, as does the pace and tone of a poem.

What has the power of inspiration to do with all this discussion of the use of devices? Inspiration, or where the poem starts, is merely where you begin. Just as the painter mixes his paints and orders his mind ready to tackle a picture, so the poet has to get to the kernel of the idea, and convey a concept through the manipulation of words and phrases.

The theme of your poem has to be highlighted in the best possible ways, and all the devices discussed in this book are at your disposal. Remember, it is how something is said that will make the impact in a poem. To speak of devices and techniques is to make the writing of poetry seem purely academic. Consider them as aids to communication, your basic idea will appear stronger if it is helped by the use of certain methods, provided that these are used with subtlety.

13
REVISION

My dictionary defines revision as 're-examine', 'alter' or 'correct'. The thought of so much additional work when writing a poem is enough to make the heart sink. However, if revision is thought of as being part of the art of making poetry work, it might not seem so arduous a task.

You will probably already have taken the first step towards revising your poem: you will have read the poem several times, and you will have put it away for an interval so that when you read it again you were more objective in your appraisal.

When reading it again, ask yourself these questions:

1: Is the emotion that first made you write the poem really being conveyed?
2: If not, what is lacking?
3: Would it help if you changed either:
the words and their meaning?
the words and their sounds?
4: Is the form you have chosen the one that works best for the subject matter?
5: Is the poem too statement-like?
6: Is it too subjective?
7: Is it too sentimental?

If you find that any of these questions are relevant, then the revision process may take longer than the original creation of the poem when you wrote down your first inspired thoughts and moulded them into some sort of pattern. The pattern originally selected may, during the revision process, prove to have been the wrong one.

When you first jotted down the basic idea that came to you, did you believe that the poem was finished? Perhaps you read it aloud to friends, or during a poetry workshop. You may have read it with all the inflections, pauses and tempos that you knew should be contained in the lines. It is easy to do this, because you know in your head how the poem should read.

It has been stated elsewhere in this book that poets need to be totally committed to the craft of creating poetry, and must ensure that what they write, conveys in the best possible way the certain something that provoked them into writing it.

Whatever happens during the revision stage, do not lose heart. It is worth persevering, and your poem will be improved and more powerful when you finish.

The structure of your poem has to be the prop for the statement, emotion or essence within it. The theme has to be the prominent feature, however, and not the structure.

Poetry has been described as being 'the thing that goes straight to the heart'. Hilaire Belloc once said: 'How is a startling of the soul produced by the collocation of a few simple sounds?'

It has been said that poets write primarily from instinct and for themselves. This is true when writing in the first frenzy, when the important thing is to grasp the idea that has come. Unfortunately, it is a common error to think of poetry as being a literal outpouring of emotion.

The origins of a poem may begin in a way that cannot be explained, and if the mystery and magical connotations that surround poetry were removed, some part of it would be lost. However, after capturing the first idea, the poem needs to be explored. Patterns and forms need to be selected carefully, so that they enhance the origin, the mystery and the power of a poem.

First of all when revising, check the words that you have used. Make sure they imply what is meant within the poem. Change them if necessary or, if it is preferred at this point, make a list of more suitable words that can be used. Select words that create imagery or music as well as defining a meaning or describing something.

Take careful note of the form selected to contain your original thought. The form may have been dictated to you as the first idea occurred, for example words that rhyme often come in a rush of thought – but these may not be the most suitable for your poem.

Take a fresh look also at the pattern of the poem, and amend it if necessary. This may perhaps be done through a syllable count, a metrical sequence, or a rhythmic pattern.

One point of revision is to leave the poem for a while. This allows the poet to view the work in a new way when returning to it. Even after a few days the poet can bring a more discerning eye to the work in hand.

When checking your work, if you feel that you have used a tone that is too strident, then correct this by making statements that are more restrained. It depends on the subject matter whether statement-like poetry is effective. Make sure that, although the voice of the poet – your own – is heard throughout the poem, this does not monopolise in a way that is aggressive, or dictatorial. Modulate your tone if this is happening, by making your observations in a subtle way.

Hyperbole – an exaggerated statement that is not meant to be taken literally – can be effective if the intention of a poet is to make a statement that is strident. It can have an urgent tone, but should only be used in minute doses.

To avoid making any declaration in a strident way, try to find an approach from which you can state your feelings. This may mean, of course, moving whole lines about at revision time, rather than a few words. Come into the poem gently, perhaps through the medium of dialogue, do not overdescribe, and leave some of your feelings for the reader to gauge.

The process of re-examining and correcting is often undertaken by poets as they progress into the poem being worked on, so that at revision time some amendments have already been made. However, a complete reappraisal undertaken when it is felt a poem is finished can prove valuable.

It is difficult, of course, to know when a poem is actually finished. It is again a case where instinct must be the guiding factor. The criterion that helps me is to assume a poem is complete when any more alterations would detract from the magical something, that impulse that brought it into being and which is at the heart of the poem, would be lost.

Revision allows time for the poet to assess whether the true depth and quality of a poem has been attained. We have, in this chapter, covered some of the things that might be looked at during revision, and one of these is whether a poet has been too subjective. This is difficult; poetry is, after all, made up from personal thoughts and emotions.

In attempting to retain an impression of what may seem to be an earth-shattering experience, it is easy to narrate the incident in the first person. Nothing wrong with that, but something entirely based on a personal outlook that may not be sufficiently objective can appear an indulgence, a letting loose of feelings that at the very least hint at being egotistical.

It is not suggested that material of a subjective nature should never be used. One has only to read the sonnets of William Shakespeare and others, or the poetry of contemporary confessional poets, to realise that in the hands of those who know their craft, poetry can be moulded in the language of restraint.

Use the more restrictive forms and rhythms if you find that you are not only narrating your poem in the first person, but that you are pouring out in lines and phrases all your personal convictions and ideas. This is mere indulgence.

As well as being too subjective in a poem, it is possible to be too sentimental. Although, in any form of writing, a connection is essential between the reader and the author it is not good writing to try to achieve an excessive emotional response from readers. This is often done by simplifying reality. The sentiment, or the mental attitude that is produced by one's own feelings about something, can be reproduced by means of poetic interpretation. In other words, make the sentiment the core of your poem, and bind it in with some structure or music.

Revision can prove to be rewarding. A poem may not take on a completely new dimension, but it can be vastly improved during revision, so that it gains a new quality. Small overused words can detract from the punch of a poem's force. Note how many times you have used the words *and* or *the* in a poem.

The overuse of such words is sometimes overlooked, but during revision these and others can be checked.

If, at any point when revising, you find the work becoming tedious, then leave it for a while. Even just unwinding over a cup of tea or coffee, or by taking a brisk walk down the road, or a stroll round the garden, will do much to ease the tedium of working on a poem.

When returning to the poem after such an interval, it is possible to see with a more discerning eye those words that are repeated but do not emphasise or highlight a particular point. Search through the dictionary or thesaurus for different words. This may not seem like the act of creating poetry, but by improving the poem the original thought that motivated you to write it will become obvious to readers.

If a metrical pattern has been used, make sure that the correct pattern has been maintained in the whole poem. Check the punctuation also, try to make it work for you. This may possibly mean using enjambment, where a line roves over on to the next one without pause. This increases the pace and heightens tension. Or decide if you want a defined pause, like that of the full stop or colon. Use a dash to break or link meanings within lines. Do not forget dialogue, question, exclamation or speech marks, and the small item of apostrophes. These things can be easily overlooked during composition time, but during revision must be attended to.

Grammar can be neglected to a surprising extent during the first frenzy of inspiration. This should not be forgotten or neglected however when revising. For instance, the use of adjectives and adverbs can be overdone, these describe things and it is easy to overload poems with too much description. A poem can be weakened in this way.

Adjectives tell us which, what and how many, while adverbs explain the when, where and how. Nouns are the words or phrases used that name a person, place or thing. There are a number of good books that are helpful references with regard to grammar, and most libraries keep these in stock.

As the revision time progresses a poem may change. Lines may be altered as the poem becomes extended or moulded. The vibrations of a new musical structure may be heard. Do not neglect the voice of the poem. A poet's voice directs the viewpoint. For example a story that is related in a poem can be told through the direction of the third person, using *he* or *she* as in:

> *Downstairs he had switched on the light*
> *this way he felt that he placated the demons in*
> *the dark.*

Or perhaps the voice will tell the story from the perspective of the first person as in the example given below:

> *Inside the pentacle I sit stitching*
> *a fine seam, the softness of silk*
> *under my hands, sewing and stitching*
> *I weave my own safety, touch the silver of sadness*
> *thread it into the needle...*

Or, again the voice can be recounting certain details from the angle of the second person *you* as shown in this extract from *Family Photographs* by P. Carradice:

> *You stand, this early morning hour,*
> *at the radar cabin door.*
> *Already mud has stained your tunic*
> *and you gaze into the future...*

Sometimes the viewpoint shifts, as in the lines below taken from the same poem:

> *you look exactly what you are –*
> *well scrubbed, ambitious teacher.*
> *By contrast I am thin*
> *and reeking self indulgence.*

Just as in a story or a novel another character has been introduced.

More than one character can participate in the action or storyline of a poem. It is for the poet to decide if this works well enough for the unfolding story, and the poem as a whole. In the opening line of my poem *Interlude*, the second person perspective is prominent but another character is introduced as the poem progresses:

Already you seem removed
from this dimension,

Morning sounds outside
discourage her signifi-
cance.

Sometimes a poem can work better if it is related from the perspective of only one viewpoint, as for example in the poem below:

The Hill

The berries on rowan trees
are filled with summer blood,
and acorns drop plump to the ground.

Along, and up the hill
are strewn leaves – and small sharp twigs
– like brittle bones,
crack under my feet, as step upon step
I return to the house at the top.

And the similar houses in a row,
stand, presuming the hill conquered.

The earth is alive with secrets,
– the rowanberry
and acorn
disintegrate together.
Leaves dissolve,
sap in long stems exudes life,

the green grass of suburbia
is immaculate.

Under each new floorboard the vertebrae
of small animals lie close.

I place my feet warily,
each step a sacrilege –
each brick already a desecration.

As well as checking viewpoints at revision time, another factor that should come under careful scrutiny is that of 'time'. Shifts in time within a poem's structure, say from past to present, have to be shown as deliberate and relevant or they can appear to be grave errors of judgement on the part of the poet.

It is possible to become so closely absorbed in the writing of a poem, especially at the start of it, that such things as viewpoint and time become muddled. This is why it is essential to put the poem away for a short while after it has been written. If it is read aloud when brought out again, mistakes that had previously been overlooked will become glaringly obvious.

It is also during revision time that titles can be thought about. Sometimes a poem starts with the idea for a title. However, on other occasions titles are difficult to think of and a poem can even be left untitled. It does often add to a poem's power, however, to have a title that intrigues or offers a definition. A poem is sometimes remembered by its first line, or its title, and therefore some thought should be given to the heading.

It is a good thing to have an imaginative title. We have all seen poems simply headed *Winter*, *Springtime* or *The Storm* which does nothing to grip the interest or curiosity of a reader. It is important to search for an original idea for a title, just as it is important to think of original images and phrases within the content of the poem.

It is important not to overlook seemingly minute details when revising. For instance, the comma placed in the wrong place making a pause less effective. Or the line where, all unknowingly, you slipped from one tense to another. All these details and many others can be noted during the time of revision. At the same time a title can be changed, or one added. Titles that leap out at readers include the following:

Honeysuckle Tastes Blue
The Man Who Brought Magic
Woman in a Bright Green Hat

Titles can describe a poem, refer to a major event it describes, or to a character within it. An interesting idea is to make use of a title by making it the start of a poem. This does not mean you should write out the title and then simply use it again as the opening line. No, having thought of an unusual title then merge this into the poem, making it part of the overall concept, as this example:

Daylight
splintered
into the wintered room

This is a direct way of involving readers in a poem, although titles can of course simply give an explanation of something that is written about in the poem.

Whilst revising it is as well to note whether the visual layout of your poem is satisfactory. The lines of a poem can be the arrangement of a certain thought, and a stanza is a group of such lines. Each stanza can contain a separate thought, or be a progression of thoughts.

During revision, when taking out the unnecessary words, the content and shape of a line and stanza can change. This in turn may change the visual aspect of the poem as lines are reduced or extended. For example, if a direct statement has been made in a poem, this may well resemble a paragraph of prose. If this is not intended, try to change the statement into something that conveys the mood of the whole piece.

For instance, if the first few lines of a poem were written with the statement-like quality referred to, they might resemble the following three lines:

His look reminded me of my son,
the dark hair and eyes
were just the same.

If these were changed to something less prose like, and with merely a hint of nostalgia, the mood of the poem would be conveyed to a reader:

Dark hair and eyes, the same small smile,
reminders of the long ago

and my young son,

time is too swift...

The breaks between the lines define each thought, and the nostalgia is implied rather than stated.

What should be happening during revision is the defining of the inner sense quality of your poem, and the way a reader responds to this inner sense should be an important point to bear in mind when reworking it.

The lyrical quality of a poem may define how the lines are laid out, and this too may alter as words and lines are checked. Do not be deterred by the fact that this will involve more work, it is a necessary part of forming a complete poem.

Try to imagine the lines of your poem as being the framework for your thoughts. Some will be long, and some short and straight to the point, as ideas unfold. Remember, that long lines create a certain flow and if these add something to your poem then you might choose words that help this rhythmic effect even more.

A number of my students have been bothered by the fact that revision may remove what they consider to be the heart of their poems. They can, oddly enough, understand that revision is necessary when writing prose. The heart of a poem is often captured first of all by the instinctive use of alliteration, or a certain rhythm that is formed from a related pattern of rhyme. It is true that the heart of a poem should be captured and retained, and in the first instance this is what most poets do. The revision is part of ensuring that the main quality of a poem is retained. It is not necessary to revise so much that the first vigorous impact of a poem is lost.

My students are asked to re-examine their work and note whether any of the things they have used quite instinctively in their poems have achieved anything more than pure description or rhythmic flow. Poets should be constantly asking themselves whether what they have written from the heart can be improved on in any way. Time should be taken to decide whether any other ideas would help the poem more.

Do not, however, contrive anything simply for effect. If a poem, after a certain amount of revision, reads well, and you are sincerely convinced that nothing more can be done to improve it, then leave it at that. If a poem is manipulated too much it will appear to be false, and the words and methods you have used to explain a situation, or convey an emotion, will fail to work.

Do not forget to examine the shape of your poem when checking your work. The arrangement of lines into visual patterns is one type of shape, but shape can be formed by other means – variations in line lengths for example. If you wish to have these in a poem, the way the cadences of speech are scattered in lines will help vary each one.

Make sure, when revising, that your poem is the shape you intended it to be. A small slip in an exacting shape and pattern can make a lot of difference.

Stanzas also have a bearing on the shape of a poem, and their arrangement can be changed and improved during revision. During revision you should also check the imagery used in your poem. Does it have that vital element that makes it almost jump out at readers? If the lines in a poem lack this vital spark perhaps they are lacking in strong imagery. Be wary of using phrases that simply produce abstract images which may bring only slight impressions of the original ideas. For instance, the following lines bring only a weak interpretation of how a young child experienced joy:

The child was happy,
and laughed as he played with his friends.

The following lines give an example of something stronger than this abstract image:

joyously shrieking, you hurtle
like a clockwork toy along the path,
your upturned face illuminates the
day.

Strong or solid images can give readers something akin to a physical sensation when relating to them, and when revising a poem it is often possible to see where such devices as metaphor might make the abstract more vivid.

Question number one at the beginning of this chapter was: Is the emotion that first made you write the poem being conveyed? If after revising your poem you find that the answer to this is 'yes', then you have succeeded in what you originally set out to do. You have written a poem to the best of your ability. You have worked on it from the moment when you first knew that a poem was in your mind, right up to the stage of successful revision.

Settle back now and enjoy it. Read the poem aloud, if possible to other poets. You will be aware after revision how much of yourself has gone into it and you will be confident that you have achieved a full interpretation of your original idea.

14
Reaching Your Audience

Getting your poetry published is one way of reaching an audience. If you feel ready to send your work out for the close scrutiny of editors, then do bear in mind that on occasions there will be the inevitable rejection slips as well as success stories. If you are prepared for this, you could start with a look at the small poetry presses. There are many of these, and they are the place where many of today's established poets began. Details of these and others can be found in *The Writers' & Artists' yearbook* under the heading *Poetry Into Print*. This is published by A&C Black (Publishers) Limited, 35 Bedford Row, London WC1R 4JH.

The Small Presses and Little Magazines of UK and Ireland is a book compiled by Peter Finch and available from Oriel, The Welsh Arts Council Bookshop, The Friary, Cardiff CF1 4AA.

The *Small Press Year Book* includes a directory of over 4,000 British Small Presses. It contains a guide to making and marketing your own publication, and lists services and media contacts. Available from The Small Press Group of Britain, BM BOZO, London WC1N 3XX.

Another practical guide to getting your poetry published in magazine, pamphlet and book form is *How To Publish Your Poetry* by Peter Finch, published by Allison & Busby.

Bloodaxe Books Ltd publish the book *Getting Into Poetry* by Paul Hyland.

The Association of Little Presses located at 12 Stevenage Road, London SW6 6ES produce a helpful newsletter and catalogue (£3.00 plus 70p p&p).

For anyone requiring details of American poetry magazines, Dust Books, PO Box 100, Paradise, California 95967, publish the *Directory of Literary Magazines*.

It is always best to read through copies of magazines before submitting your work. Back copies can be obtained from most editors for the price of a single magazine plus p&p.

The Poetry Library, keeps a list of small press magazines. This is updated as far as possible but changes of magazines, editors and addresses can occur frequently. If you are unable to make the journey to the library at The Royal Festival Hall, South Bank Centre, London SE1 8XX (Tel: 071-921 0943/0664), then on receipt of a stamped sae they will forward this comprehensive list. Note, it is recommended by the Poetry Library that poets read through copies of any magazines before submitting their work.

The small presses are sometimes grant aided, but more often survive purely on a subscription basis. This does not mean that your work will be published if you become a subscriber, nor will it be rejected if you do not.

Type your poems clearly on one side of an A4 sheet, put page numbers if the poem goes over a page in length. Always enclose a stamped sae. Never fold poems more than once. Keep a file to note where you have sent poems, and the date on which they were posted. Keep a copy of each poem sent out. There are conflicting views about spacing between typed lines but it is usual to type single or one and a half spaces. Leave wide margins (if the poem is short, type it in the middle of the page) and type your name and address on the bottom of the page. Send a few poems, no more than six, so that the editor can assess your work, and do be patient.

Editors are inundated with poems, receiving so many that the task of replying promptly to individuals is well nigh impossible.

It is not wrong to send the poem to more than one editor at a time, but this can lead to confusion. If the poem is accepted by one editor, then the others need to be advised which is all time and energy consuming.

The Scottish Library is organised in a similar way to the

Poetry Library in London. It is situated at Tweedale Court, 14 High Street, Edinburgh EH1 1TE (Tel: 031-557 2876). The Northern Arts Poetry Library is located at the County Library, The Willows, Morpeth, Northumberland NE61 1TA (Tel: 0670 512385).

Regional Arts Boards can provide information on local poetry groups, workshops and societies which may help with the promotion and publication of your work. Details of these boards are available (on receipt of the usual stamped sae) from: The Arts Council of Great Britain, 14 Great Peter Street, London SW1P 3NQ.

The Poetry Society publishes *Poetry News* as their newsletter and this includes details of poetry events and festivals. Their other publication, *Poetry Review*, is issued quarterly. The Society produces the BP Teachers Resources File, and administrates the W.H. Smith Poets In Schools scheme.

It additionally handles the enormous task of running the National Poetry Competition. Details of their critical service as well as a free information pack on How To Get Your Work Published as well as a list of conferences/courses/seminars where poetry is included on the programme can be obtained if you send a stamped sae to: 22 Betterton Street, London WC2 9BU (Tel: 071-240 4810).

Poetry competitions are held regularly throughout the country, prizes range from book tokens to small or large sums of money. The prizewinning poems are sometimes published at the end of a competition, which is an added incentive for entering. The Poetry Library will send a list of these poetry competitions on receipt of the required stamped sae. This list is compiled from information provided by the organisers of the competitions.

The Arvon Foundation Courses will send brochures on request. If you do apply for information from them send a stamped sae. Write either to:- Arvon Foundation, Lumb Bank, Hebden Bridge, West Yorkshire HX7 6DF, or to: Arvon Foundation, Totleigh Barton, Sheepwash, Beaworthy, Devon EX21 5NS.

For information on the Ty Newydd Residential Writing Courses, apply (with sae) to: TY Newydd, Llanystumdwy,

Cricieth, Gwynedd LL52 0LW.

You can learn a great deal about writing poetry on these courses, but there are other advantages. You will meet other poets, and will be able to read aloud your own work during discussions and workshops. This is valuable experience, and will help you to gain confidence about reading your work before an audience. A directory of Writers Circles is compiled by J. Dick. Contact: Oldacre, Hordens Park Road, Chapel-en-le-Frith, Derbyshire.

An 'Accent on Poetry' weekend, held each May in Derbyshire, is informal yet instructive. Details on receipt of a sae from: Mr L. Richardson, Crossfields, Upper Poppleton, York YO2 6JR.

The monthly magazine *Writers News*, which gives details of writers circles around the country also includes information about many of the courses, festivals, competitions and seminars that are held around the country. This magazine, popular with writers has regular and helpful features on all aspects of writing including poetry and its address has already been given.

Radios 3 and 4 produce poetry programmes which include the work of established poets. As well as these programmes, many local radio stations include poetry and it is worth contacting your nearest local radio station to enquire whether they broadcast poetry features. Give the producer some details concerning your publications, or any information about poetry readings you may have been involved in. If your poetry is about the area where you live mention this, as it may be of interest to the producer. Watch out for poetry competitions that may be organised by radio stations or tv.

When you have had some of your work published or included in anthologies you probably would like to have a collection of your own work produced. The Poetry Library and The Poetry Society both produce lists of poetry publishers. The Poetry Society's Advice and Information Service produces a list of the major poetry publishers as well as offering advice on such matters as copyright and fees. By all means try the big names first, including Faber & Faber or Chatto & Windus. It is more likely, though, that your collection will be produced once you have gained recognition by being well published in magazines and small presses. Having said that, however, who knows? Your poetry may be just what the big names are looking for.

You can of course self-publish your own book. This is not to be confused with vanity publishing.

If at this stage you have a ready market place for your work (perhaps a school or an association for whom you give regular talks) or you have a society willing to set up a venue where you could sell your books, then go ahead and publish. A book that is available to help you is Peter Finch's *How to Publish Yourself* published by Allison & Busby.

You will have to attend to all the details that publishers usually take off your hands. The matter of obtaining an ISBN (International Standard Book Number) for instance, and making certain that the copyright libraries receive the necessary six copies. You will also have to distribute and sell your own books.

Now to the matter of vanity publishing. Avoid this at all costs, and 'costs' is the operative word. You will have to pay for your poems to be produced in a book that is not edited or checked. The distribution will most likely be left to you. The book will not be taken seriously by editors, and consequently will not be reviewed. Do not therefore answer the advertisements that pander to our vanities claiming for example: 'publisher seeks poetry for publication'. Genuine publishers usually have many more poems sent to them than they can deal with.

There is a market for poetry that is referred to as 'light'. This exists in the pages of a number of the magazines that are published for women.

The short poems written for greetings cards may prove another outlet for your work. If you are interested in this style check with the writing yearbooks in the reference section of your local library.

Keep writing, and send your poems out to different editors, different magazines and publications. Determination and perseverance will, hopefully, help you to become established.

ACKNOWLEDGEMENTS AND THANKS

Chatto & Windus and the Estate of Wilfred Owen for permission to reproduce an extract from the poem *Strange Meeting* by Wilfred Owen from *The Poems of Wilfred Owen* 1931.

Faber & Faber for permission to reproduce an extract from the poem *The Rabbit Catcher* by Sylvia Plath from the book *Winter Trees* © Ted Hughes 1971, and for permission to reproduce an extract from the poem *Autobiography* by Louis MacNeice from *The Collected Poems of Louis MacNeice* edited by E.R. Dodds.

Joan Woodcock for her poem *For Spring* from her book *Borrowing From Time* published by Envoi Poets Publications.

Phil Carradice for his poem *Burma Star* and extracts from his poem *Family Photographs* from the anthology *The Unsaid Goodnight* published by Stride.

Barbara Rennie for her poem *The Reading* (Irina Ratushkinskaya London May 12th 1987) from her book *As If* published by Envoi Poets Publications.

Jean Marian Stevens for her poem *Music* from her book *Led by Kingfishers* published by Outposts Publications.

Anita Marie Sackett for her poem *Cowslips* published by *Scholastic Collections: Poetry compiled by Wes Magee* (under the changed title of *Grandma*).

Anne Lewis-Smith for her poem *Gift of a Snail Shell* published by Envoi Poets Publications their Summer Anthology 1990.

J. Michael Sharman for his poem *Intrusions*.

Susan Skinner for her poem *Monet's Garden* from her book of that title published by Headland.

Susan James for her poem *Disorder Discourse* published by The Alison House Poets Collection edited by Robin Gregory.

Ian Emberson for his poem *The Barn in Summer* from his book *Swallows Return.*

Alison Chisholm for her poem *Last Day* from her book *Paper Birds* published by Stride.

Graeme L. Jennens for his poem *Poetic Lamentations.*

Ceinwen Sanderson for her poem *Boatrace.*

Victoria Kingsley for her poem *Crank* from the anthology *Galaxy of Grandmothers Contemporary Verse* published by Phoenix Poets, London, edited by Arda Lacey.

Frank J. Dullaghan for his haiku examples.

Arda Lacey for her limerick.

Arthur Stump for clerihew example.

Margaret Pain for her poem *Gift* from her book *No Dark Legend* published by Hub.

Peggy Poole for her poem *Ebb Tide* from her book *Hesitations* and Envoi Poets Publications Summer Anthology 1990.

Leslie Richardson for his poem *The Ringing of Pigs* and an extract from his poem *Celebration* from his book *The Spade of my Father* published by Littlewood Press.

Beryl Cross for her poem *Sussex Drought*, published in Envoi magazine.

Brenda Whincup for her poem *Feet First.*

Alison Bielski for her poem *In My Dreamfield* from the anthology *The Unsaid Goodnight* published by Stride.

Roger Elkin for his poem *Omaha Beach* published in Literary Olympians II (USA) and for permission to quote from his article on free verse published in *Envoi* 102.

To the staff of The Poetry Library and The Poetry Society for all their help.

INDEX